Jamie Pennell has had an esteemed eighteen-year career as a soldier and leader inside the New Zealand SAS. He was sent on multiple operations and deployed four times to Afghanistan to assist other nations and the Afghan special forces in the war on terror. After leaving the Defence Force, Jamie worked with high performance athletes where he helped them achieve their sporting goals. Jamie now works as the head of Dilworth School's outdoor programme at their Mangatāwhiri campus, training young men in skills for life.

SERVICEMAN J

JAMIE
PENNELL

HarperCollins*Publishers*

HarperCollins*Publishers*
Australia • Brazil • Canada • France • Germany • Holland • India
Italy • Japan • Mexico • New Zealand • Poland • Spain • Sweden
Switzerland • United Kingdom • United States of America

First published in 2024
by HarperCollins*Publishers* (New Zealand) Limited
Unit D1, 63 Apollo Drive, Rosedale, Auckland 0632, New Zealand
harpercollins.co.nz

A catalogue record for this book is available from the National Library of New Zealand

ISBN 978 1 7755 4238 4 (paperback)
ISBN 978 1 7754 9269 6 (ebook)
ISBN 978 1 4607 3876 4 (audiobook)

Written with Nicola McCloy and edited by Kimberley Davis
Cover design by Louisa Maggio, HarperCollins Design Studio
Front cover image by Pedro Ugarte / AFP
Back cover image by shutterstock.com
Typeset in Sabon LT Std by Kirby Jones
Printed and bound in Australia by McPherson's Printing Group

MIX
Paper | Supporting
responsible forestry
FSC® C001695

To my son, who brings out the best in me.
May this book inspire you to be your amazing self and
make your mark on the world.

CONTENTS

CONTENTS

INTRODUCTION

JUST BEFORE 10 O'CLOCK on the morning of 18 January 2010, a man walked towards the main gate of Afghanistan's central bank on Pashtunistan Square in Kabul. When the guards told him to stop, he continued walking towards them. And, when they drew their weapons and shot at him, his suicide vest exploded.

Pashtunistan Square is in the middle of a big roundabout, not far from the Presidential Palace and opposite the Serena Hotel, and this was the first of several attacks to take place near the square that day. Shortly afterwards, two more men blew themselves up in a nearby shopping centre, while others fired grenades into the Ministry of Finance building. Meanwhile, still more moved into buildings that bordered the roundabout and started firing down towards the Presidential Palace.

We got word of what was happening within about 20 minutes, and immediately geared up, climbed into our Land

Cruisers and followed the Crisis Response Unit (CRU) into the city centre. While in Afghanistan, we'd been mentoring and training the CRU, and it was our job that day to support them in their operations and make sure they were taking the lead.

The traffic on the way in was gridlocked, but the lights and sirens on our vehicles got us through quickly. When we arrived at the square we could hear the gunshots – but we couldn't quite figure out where the shooters were. In the middle of the square, some Afghan army or police members were cowering behind a big rock while being shot at from one of the buildings. We had to get over there. So, one at a time, we sprinted across the roundabout. There was a lot of shooting going on. It was absolute carnage. As we tried to get a gauge on what was happening, someone fired shots down the street in our direction. Some of our group took cover behind cars, while a few others and I went around the corner. Still trying to work out what was going on, I poked my head out, and *boomphah!* A bullet went straight past my head. Way too close.

Eventually, we noticed some bullet exit holes in the mirrored-glass window of a building about 200 metres down the road. So that's where our shooter was hiding. We tried to get a bead on him, but he kept changing positions, and there was so much stuff going on and so many people moving about that we couldn't just lay down fire. Then we saw some other military – possibly the Afghan National Army (ANA) – running towards his position, so we left them to deal with him and turned our attention to the others. It was going to be hard to clear them all out, because the buildings where they were hiding were so solid; internal and external walls made of concrete meant every room was a bunker. This country had been living in a state of war for so long that gunshots and bombs had become the norm, and all the buildings were strengthened beyond what would usually be required.

We saw the Afghan commandos – Task Force 333, trained by British advisors – arrive from down south and start making their way across the rooftops to a building across the street. Meanwhile, we started making our way around the building. First a grenade got thrown out of a window at us and blew up nearby, then we heard a really big blast go off further down the street. A suicide bomber had driven what looked like an ambulance up to the cordon, been waved through by the Afghan National Police (ANP), then driven the van to the nearby Gulbahar shopping mall and *boom!* He'd detonated about 100 kilos of explosives.

There were cars everywhere and fire engines coming straight through the cordon. I glanced warily at all the cars we were standing so close to. *If one of them goes off*, I thought, *we're dead*. So we moved away from the street, and the CRU started to work their way through the buildings, trying to figure out where all the attackers were. Meanwhile, I stayed down at street level, as this gave me a better over-watch position from which to coordinate things. Then I looked around to find a camera in my face. It was a reporter, and he was bang smack in the middle of us, trying to snap pictures while also using us as protection.

'Hey!' I said. 'What are you doing in here?'

'Oh, no, it's all right,' he said. 'I'm just trying to figure out what's going on.'

It wasn't all that unusual for there to be journalists in the thick of the action. It seemed like the media always got to events before the military – that was why CNN or Fox News was always on in the ops room back at camp. Journos tended to be based in the middle of the city, and they had people all over listening and informing them of whatever was going on. Within 20 minutes of something happening, they'd be reporting it on the international news networks. But I couldn't believe the audacity of this guy. One of my guys grabbed his camera and cleared it, then handed it back.

'Mate, get out of here,' I said. 'We're not here to protect you.'

*

Eventually, the commandos inside the buildings located and engaged the last two shooters, but once the Americans at street level started using a mounted 50 cal as fire support towards the second floor at close range, I pulled my guys out. I didn't want them getting hit by ricochets. Not worth losing any lives with that going on.

The attacks unfolded over a couple of hours, and the Taliban ultimately claimed responsibility for them. All up about 20 people were killed that day, and more than 70 injured, and it took a while for things to calm down afterwards.

Once the buildings were cleared, another SAS soldier and I went over to have a look at them inside. We were walking back out again when Willie said to me, 'Hey, mate, I think we're being photographed.' It was the same journalist from earlier – and, this time, he was *definitely* taking photos of us.

Within hours, one photo in particular had been published internationally. In New Zealand, it caused a bit of a stir. I still had my helmet on so couldn't be identified, but Willie had taken his off. And he was very recognisable. A few years earlier, he'd become the first recipient of the Victoria Cross for New Zealand. Everyone at home knew who Willie Apiata was, even if they didn't recognise me.

*

Who dares wins. That's the motto of the NZSAS, the special forces unit of Ngāti Tūmatauenga/the New Zealand Army. 'If you think you have supreme commitment and self-discipline,' says the Defence Careers website, 'this may be the career path for you.'

Four guiding tenets underpin everything that the regiment does, and those in the unit refer back to them time and time again. As members of the regiment, you are expected to have an unrelenting pursuit of excellence, maintain the highest standard of discipline, 'brook no sense of class' (to believe in complete equality among your comrades regardless of rank or where they come from), and always approach challenges with humour and humility. There's also one other, very important guiding principle: you can't talk about what you do to anyone outside of the regiment. Not about operations, not identities, not tactics, not techniques, not equipment. Nothing. It's called Operational Security, or OPSEC, and it's what protects who we are and what we do. In fact, the only people you can really talk to about life in the regiment are your fellow SAS soldiers.

A lot of people seem to have a certain perception about the regiment. They think we're cold-hearted, knuckle-dragging gorillas who just go out there and wipe people off the face of the Earth. The reality couldn't be further from the truth.

As well as making it through a gruelling nine-day selection course then an eleven-month cycle of training, you need to demonstrate high levels of intelligence, skill and integrity to get into the regiment – and the longer you stay, the higher those levels are expected to be. You're always under the microscope. You've got to work really well both individually and as part of a team. You've got to be able to make well-considered decisions quickly. And you've got to be tough mentally. The regiment needs to know that, if they're sending you away by yourself, then your mission is going to be achieved, no matter what. It's tough. That's the job.

Grinding all day long with the pack on your back is the easy part. That's just one foot in front of the other, and you can block everything out. But that's just one part of the challenge. That's the grit. The other part? That comes when you no longer have the pack on, when you're by yourself, isolated, and have to talk to those voices in your head. Working that part out takes another type of mental toughness and, for me – as for many servicepeople like me – it also took time.

*

When I discovered that photo of Willie and me had made it to the front pages, it was a weird feeling. I might have had my helmet on, but those who knew me and Willie put two and two together. The public didn't recognise me, but some of my acquaintances did. That was strange, given hardly anyone knew where I was or what I was doing. Even my family knew very little – just when I was being deployed, but nothing else.

The then-prime minister John Key criticised the local media for publishing the photo. 'A high level of secrecy around the SAS is needed,' he said. 'We don't want [the Taliban and Al-Qaeda] to know the names and individual identities of members of the SAS ... It puts at risk the lives of those individual soldiers because they can now be recognised.'

Then, a year and a bit after that, in 2011, the same thing happened again. Another photograph of me hit the country's front pages. This time, though, my face was blurred out, and the picture was accompanied by headlines such as 'NZ soldiers play "major role" in Kabul hotel firefight'.

Afterwards, the New Zealand government announced that two of the servicepeople involved in that hotel incident had been awarded the nation's second-highest military award – the New Zealand Gallantry Star. Both were serving members of the SAS at the time, and neither was publicly identified, but the citation for one read:

Serviceman J demonstrated outstanding gallantry and leadership under heavy fire from a determined enemy, contributing to the resolution of the incident and the protection of comrades and civilian life. Serviceman J's performance was of the highest order and in keeping with the finest traditions of New Zealand's military record.

I am Serviceman J.

1

WARTS AND ALL

I WAS JUST 17 when I filled out an application to join the army. On the last page was a question along the lines of 'What are your aspirations?' and in response I wrote 'To join the SAS'. I didn't know anything about the SAS back then beyond the fact that they were based out at Hobsonville, west of Auckland. But, as it turned out, I wasn't quite old enough to join the army anyway. 'Wait another year, then try again,' they told me.

That year went by, and I left school and got a full-time job at an engineering-parts company. My boss put a lot of faith in me, talking about enrolling me to do a certificate in engineering, then making me a sales rep after that. I was really committed to my career with him, and I forgot all about my army plans.

Then one afternoon I got a phone call after work. I was 19 by then. It was an army recruiter, and he'd got my number from that application I'd done while I was still at school.

He was calling to tell me that 30-odd people had come off basic training and he was looking for people to replace them. 'I'll give you an hour to make a decision,' he said. 'In the meantime, I'll be ringing around a whole lot of others to see if I can fill the gaps.' Then, before hanging up, he added: 'If it's a yes when I call you back, you'll need to be ready to go down to Waiouru the day after tomorrow.'

I was really torn. What should I do? Stay in my job, or chuck everything in and join the army? So I called Mum. But she just said, 'It's not up to me. It's up to you.'

I was a bit disappointed. This was one of those situations where I'd hoped Mum would tell me what to do. After she and my father divorced when I was eight, I ended up living with her. I have two sisters, but they're quite a bit older than me, so for most of the time at home it was just me and Mum. All of the women in my family are strong, so I've been around that sort of strength all my life.

'What do *you* want to do, Jamie?' Mum asked me. 'You've always talked about the army, but it's a big decision. It really is up to you.'

And that actually helped me to make up my mind. When the recruiter called back – exactly one hour later – I told him I was good to go. Then I called my boss and informed him I was off to join the army.

*

Mum took the following day off work and we went shopping. She bought me a suit, a toilet bag and all of the gear on the equipment list that the recruiter had given me. Then I called in at work to say goodbye. And the day after that, I was in a van, on my way from Auckland down to Waiouru.

About four hours later, we hit the Desert Road, and as if on cue it started snowing. From the moment the van pulled up at Waiouru Military Camp just half an hour later, it was all on. 'Get out of the van!' some guy was shouting. 'Form up! Get into line, you little shits!' We were marched straight off down to the admin office. 'As soon as you sign the line, you're mine!' the guy in there said.

I was reeling from the sudden change of scene, but I was also excited. Two days earlier, joining the army hadn't even been on my mind. It was maybe a possibility in the distant future, but not immediately, and now here I was. I'd had no time to prepare myself.

For a moment, I wondered whether I really wanted to be going down this track after all.

*

The rest of the guys on basic training had already been there for about a week and a half, so they were reasonably well integrated into army life. I was definitely one of the new boys on the block.

On my second or third night, one of the corporals lined the whole platoon up in the corridor. 'Stand to attention,' he ordered. He was a big guy, but his voice was surprisingly soft. 'Some of you characters look weak,' he said. 'Who's taken a punch before?'

I'd been doing martial arts since I was a kid. My uncle was a black belt in karate, and he'd got me into it when I was about eight. I was always bouncing about, so the physicality of it was great for me. Then, when I was ten, I started doing jiu-jitsu too, and a couple of years later I got into Muay Thai (Thai boxing), as one of the top gyms in the country, Balmoral Lee Gar, was near where we lived. They had Ray Sefo and Jason Suttie fighting there at the time, and Lolo Heimuli was the trainer. He was the man – still is! I trained there until I joined the army. So, yes, I'd taken plenty of punches ... but there was no way I was going to mention any of this to the softly spoken corporal.

A few people did pipe up to claim they had, but the corporal just carried on. 'You all look like babies,' he said. 'Stay standing to attention. I'm going to toughen you up by giving you each a punch in the stomach.'

He started making his way along the row. *Bam! Bam! Bam!* Giving each guy a big punch, and gradually drawing nearer ... But when he punched me, he didn't hit the spot. I wasn't winded. But I still doubled over, pretending that he'd got me. I didn't want to get another one from him.

'Get up, Pennell, you wimp!' he said before moving on to the next guy.

From then on, I knew I wasn't living with Mum anymore. This was back in the nineties, when that sort of physical punishment was still going on in the army. Things were about to change, though – even two years later, you wouldn't have seen that sort of thing happening. In fact, by then people were getting kicked out of the army for it. It's a good thing, too, as I saw quite a few people negatively affected by that kind of behaviour.

*

When we arrived in Waiouru, we had to choose a regiment to join. I was young, and I had no idea what I wanted to do, so I picked my top three: chef, engineer, infantry – in that order. In my mind, being a chef or an engineer would have given me a trade, while the infantry would mean I'd get to be a frontline soldier. I ended up in the infantry, and my fate was sealed. (And I know now that pretty much anyone who put 'infantry' anywhere on their list ended up there!)

Basic training lasted three months, and while we were learning how to be soldiers, I was also trying to figure out who my cohort was, and who I could trust. There were some bullies in there, so I had to stand up for myself, but everything settled down soon enough. Everyone was doing the same stuff, and all the challenges presented to us – mental, physical or emotional – helped to sort things out. Usually, if someone was being mouthy or trying to act tough, they'd end up getting schooled because someone else was faster than them or better at the set tasks. As the playing field evened out, we gained collective respect for each other's strengths, while coming to understand each other's weaknesses as well. We had a pretty good cohort, and I made friends for life in that group.

Once we completed basic training, we moved from Waiouru to Linton Military Camp, just outside Palmerston North. There, we went into infantry corps training, and after I passed that and got my infantry red diamond, I joined the 1st Battalion, Royal New Zealand Infantry Regiment.

*

While I was at camp, I managed to hold my temper and not kick off at my superiors, no matter what they threw at me. The same could not be said for my life off base, however. I definitely got more aggressive after I joined the army. They were pulling it out of me, and it was a classic case of work hard, play hard.

In Palmerston North, there were all sorts – university students, rugby teams, gangs and us army boys – and we'd all be out drinking on Friday and Saturday nights. The Square, in the city's heart, didn't have any lighting back then. We used to deliberately walk through there at 11 or 12pm and go one at a time, and it would just happen. I think I had more street fights in Palmerston North than I had fights in the ring. Those fights could have easily got any of us into a whole heap of trouble, but we were young and spoiling for a spar. None of us were thinking very far into the future.

The infantry battalions were so prone to mischief that, as well as the military police, we had our own regimental police. They'd come into town and drive around Palmerston North just to keep an eye on us all.

When I'd been in the battalion about a year, I applied and was accepted to go on the selection course for the SAS. By now I knew a bit more about the SAS, and I'd decided I wanted to join. Honestly, I think I always did. I knew it was going to be hard, so I'd sussed out a training plan and got started. I could have approached the physical training instructors at Linton Gym to help me with my training, but for some reason I didn't.

Then, about six weeks before the selection course started, I went into town and got on the piss with some of the boys. We came back to Linton around two in the morning, turned the radio on, grabbed some beers and carried on with the party – even though we weren't allowed to drink in the barracks.

Then we heard someone banging on the door. 'Open up! This is the orderly sergeant!'

Instead of doing as we were told, we just turned the radio off and sat there in silence. We were trying to pretend we weren't here. 'Don't say anything,' one of my mates whispered.

It didn't occur to us that the regimental police might work out that the radio didn't switch itself off ...

'I know you guys are in there,' the sergeant said. 'Now open the door!'

'Hey,' I whispered to my mates. 'I'll go out the window.' We were two storeys up, and when I opened the window and looked down, I locked eyes with the orderly corporal. He was standing on the ground floor.

'Open the door,' he said.

Busted.

We opened the door, and the sergeant came straight in. 'You guys are all on charge,' he said.

We all ended up in front of the commanding officer (CO), who gave us each 28 days confined to barracks. That meant that, from five in the morning until ten at night, our free time belonged to the army. They'd make us turn up in our best dress, then five minutes later run us out in our combat dress. They'd pull our packs apart and put everything out on the ground, then we'd have to run one item at a time back to the barracks. We spent hours running backwards and forwards. We cleaned, painted rocks, ran across the confidence course in our dress uniforms.

It was 28 days of chaos that just happened to lead up to my SAS selection course.

*

The purpose of the SAS selection course is to demonstrate an individual soldier's performance carrying out the highest function of a SAS soldier at the standard the SAS sets. They want to see you warts and all. You can't hide anything, no matter how hard you try.

So, what does that look like? You have to be able to carry a heavy load (pack, webbing and rifle) day and night, regardless of season, weather or terrain. You have to function when deprived of sleep and food. You have to be able to navigate with a map and compass over long distances from checkpoint to checkpoint. You're put under time pressure, given no support and must operate within strict control measures over a week and a half. You don't get any form of input, positive or negative; you just get instructions of what to do.

Despite what TV shows can make these sorts of selection courses look like, there's no yelling at candidates. That's not an SAS thing. That's because the regiment members running the course shouldn't have to yell at anyone. If a person needs to be yelled at to be motivated, then they probably don't belong there. To be an SAS soldier, you have to be intrinsically motivated. You have to be able to manage yourself.

The selection course is hard, and it's meant to be. A pass is by no means guaranteed, no matter how fit or experienced or tough you think you are. Candidates who are athletic, strong and muscular often fail selection, while the skinny guys make it through. There's no standard body type or sort of person in the regiment, and it's a cross-section of society –farmers, engineers, lawyers, military, whatever. Each person brings their strengths to the fore at different points in time. That's how the SAS achieves its missions.

To identify someone as being in the SAS is very difficult – and so it should be.

*

Prior to the selection course actually starting, there was a week and a half of build-up training. During this time, all 70 of us did a bit of navigation training, went over how to use radios, reviewed our gear and did a whole lot of other bits and pieces to get us up to speed. We also did some psych tests.

Then, on the morning of the day that the selection course actually began, we had our last full breakfast. From that moment on, for as long as we were on the course, breakfast consisted of one sausage, one egg, a tablespoon of baked beans, maybe a piece of toast and a cup of tea (no sugar). That was all. After that, we'd go all day without any lunch. Dinner, if we were lucky, was a 200ml cup of watered-down soup (maybe less) and a piece of bread.

Our food wasn't the only thing deliberately restricted throughout the selection process. Our sleep and our movements were also controlled, and this had a psychological effect on a lot of people. Food (and sleep) deprivation are real considerations on operations, when you're not always going to have three square meals a day. This process helped to weed out the dreamers, and in some ways it put the smaller guys at an advantage because they had less muscle to feed.

The first day of selection is basically a conditioning day, designed to deplete candidates' energy. Basically, you do all the army fitness tests in one day. First is the required fitness-level test: a 2.4-kilometre run, push-ups, sit-ups and pull-ups. That's followed by the battle efficiency test: carrying a 30-kilogram pack 12 kilometres. Then you came back and do a fireman's carry, jump a ditch, climb a 1.8-metre wall, go up and down a rope with your webbing on, and finish with a casualty carry. After that, it's into the pool to do a swim test where, as well as swimming, you have to do a rescue tow and a retrieval off the bottom of the pool.

The final test of the day is what's known as 'hounds and hares': an 8-kilometre run in your fatigues, boots and webbing, carrying your rifle. You have to chase the 'hare' and try not to be caught by the 'hounds'. One of the badged guys just starts running – he's the hare – and behind the candidate come the hounds – badged regiment members sweeping the back of the course. When I did it, the guy at the front was going at a speed that not many people could keep up with – remember we'd just done all those fitness tests, with only 30 minutes to recover between each. The hounds went at a minimum pace, but just kept going.

By the end of it all, we were all absolutely zonked.

*

Back at barracks that evening, we ate our meagre dinner then eventually went to sleep on our thermal mats on the floor. In those days, they were allowed to keep you awake for as long as they wanted, but that's since changed – now you get a minimum amount of sleep, maybe five or six hours. When I did the selection course, though, we were kept up until midnight or one in the morning, and even when we did sleep it was in the knowledge that we could be woken at any time. We took whatever time we were given to sleep, woke up in the morning, and then it was back at it.

The next morning after breakfast, we got on the trucks and were driven 120 kilometres south from Hobsonville to Limestone Downs. Whenever we were on the truck, there was always a badged member with us. No one was allowed to talk or go to sleep. We had to be in full control at all times, and that was quite crushing for some people.

At Limestone Downs, we embarked on three days of open-country navigation, and covered anywhere between 30 and 40 kilometres a day. The routes were point to point, and you had to work out the best track from checkpoint A to B to C to D.

The track you chose determined how long you were out there for, but there was also an overall time limit. To get in under this time limit, you had to move fast and be smart about your route, all while carrying a 30-kilogram load. Basically, you could walk up the hills, but you had to run on the flats and downhills or you'd be facing a fail. To get through these three days, you had to be both internally driven and unworried by the suffering you experienced.

It was during these first four days that the most people dropped off. There were various reasons people didn't make it. Sometimes, they decided to pull off. If that was the case, they were given five minutes to think about their decision. Then one of the badged guys would ask them again if they still wanted to pull off and if they said yes, they'd get sent back to the truck.

Other times, people had the decision to pull off made for them. That could be because they'd failed to make the timings for the day, or maybe they'd broken the rules, or possibly they were deemed medically unfit to continue. Often the guys who were injured didn't want to leave the course. They'd just keep going until it became clear that they weren't going to make the cut-off times. They weren't going to quit, so someone else had to make the call for them.

People were dropping out all the time – but not me. Not yet. I made it through the open-country navigation reasonably comfortably, and that brought me to my next challenge: Exercise von Tempsky, aka the jerry-can carry. This exercise gets its official name from Gustavus von Tempsky, who led the colonial Forest Rangers during the New Zealand Wars, and even those of us who were first-timers on the selection course knew it was a bit of a barrier test. When you make it to von Tempsky, that's when things start to get real.

We were put into groups of five and given six 20-litre jerry cans. We were already carrying our packs, webbing and rifles, but we had to make sure that all six of those jerry cans were carried for the next 20 hours. To make that happen, we each carried one can and took turns lugging the extra one. You could let your can touch the ground for moments while the group rotated and you had a drink, but that was it. When a person dropped out, they took their jerry can with them, and the rest of you carried those that remained.

The exercise was held in the sand dunes out at Muriwai Beach, on the coast west of Auckland, and we were pointed in one direction and told to get going. Our instructions: 'Walk that way for ten hours, then turn around and come back.' The idea was to go all day and right through the night. It's an activity that's replicated on operations.

This was the point when I realised I wasn't as fit as I needed to be. I made it ten hours in before I hit the wall. I simply didn't have the physical capacity to complete the task. I pulled off the course.

There was a lot of shame in failing to make it through selection. I had to turn around and go back to Linton, back to the battalion. But, instead of taking this failure as a sign that the regiment wasn't for me, I used it as fuel to prepare me for another attempt.

I decided I was going to come back in a year's time.

2

TICK OR FLICK

WHEN I TURNED UP at selection at the end of the following year, I felt more ready than I'd ever be. I was really driven to succeed, mostly because I didn't want to fail again. For some, the fear of failure stops them from trying, but for me it was motivating.

Back at Linton, I'd gone from the rifle company into Mortar Platoon, Support Coy, and our platoon that year had been a bit of an exception in the sense that everyone was really fit. We'd ended up winning the Battalion Section Skill at Arms, which is essentially a competition between all the sections in the battalion. At the same time, I'd also done a six-week Assistant Physical Training Instructor (APTI) course, which was timed pretty well, as it finished roughly a month before SAS selection started. By the end of that course, I was as fit as I've ever been.

Outside of work, I'd also sharpened up and made sure to stay out of trouble. No more fighting on the streets. Instead,

I got into boxing at the local gym and started having a few fights in the ring, and that helped me steer clear of any more street-fighting mischief.

I chose to go for summer selection in November. You can choose either summer or winter, but neither is particularly advantageous – although more people drop out on the days when it's really hot. I chose summer because, if I passed, it meant I'd get to go back to battalion, pack my gear and I'd start official training in January the next year.

I went into that selection with a mindset that the only way I'd get pulled off would be if I was seriously injured, incapacitated or dead. There was no way I was going to fail any of the activities – they would have to physically pull me off selection to get me to stop.

It was now or never.

*

Once again I made it through the open-country navigation, and this year I did it pretty easily. A lot of the stuff was painful, but it definitely helped that I was so fit. I saw plenty of others self-sabotaging, though, by getting a bit emotional about their physical state – their feet, their knees, their back, their hips, their shoulders, their neck, their brain. There were some really top-quality soldiers from my unit on the course with me, including a senior soldier in the battalion. He was someone I held in high regard, so I was surprised to find him sitting on the side of the track one day. When I stopped to ask what he was doing, he replied, 'Oh … I'm going to pull off.'

'But there's a checkpoint coming up,' I said. 'Just keep going.'

'Nah,' he said. 'It's not for me.'

I stood there toing and froing with him for a couple of minutes before finally making the call to leave him. He'd given up, but I hadn't. *I'm supposed to be junior to this guy,* I thought as I walked away, *but I'm the one who's still here.*

Seeing others fall off can shake a person's confidence. It can take you out. The doubt creeps in, and you start to think, *If that guy can't do it, then I probably won't be able to either* … And then it's all but over for you, too. That's not what happened for me. Every time I saw someone leaving while I stayed, I drew energy from it. I started to feel more confident in my own abilities. *I am supposed to be here,* I began to realise.

I was hungry and tired, just like everyone else, but I'd wake up each day and find the energy to keep going. I knew I could do the physical part, so I focused on my headspace. I concentrated on making it through each day's task. *I'm going to get to the end of this,* I'd think, *and I'm going to make it in time.*

That's what I needed to do, so it's what I focused on doing, task by task and day by day.

*

Then I came to the test that had ended my SAS dream the year before: the jerry-can carry. This time round, though, I was going to die before I dropped out of the exercise.

We didn't have watches, but every hour there'd be a couple of minutes' break so we could put our cans down, shuffle the extra one between us and grab a drink. On each of these breaks, I'd think, *Cool, just done another hour.* And I'd focus on making it to the next one.

Some time during the wee hours, I started hallucinating. I would close my eyes and see a fluorescent brain. Then I started seeing things out of the corner of my eyes, too. The bushes were moving, and there was a silver ball that kept flashing across the ground in front of me like I was in a giant pinball machine.

I ignored it all. No matter what happened or what I saw, I was determined to just keep putting one foot in front of the other.

I made it to hour ten, and kept going.

Hour eleven. I'd passed the barrier I'd hit the year before. Over halfway.

Nine hours left … eight … seven …

I was getting closer …

I saw the sun coming up. *There's no way I'm getting off now.*

By this point, everyone was just destroyed. We were all shuffling along, doing our best to simply keep moving. Some people tried to undo the cap of their jerry cans and let some of the water out, but they all got caught. Then they'd be loaded up with even more, and they'd really know about it.

Finally, I hit the 20-hour mark. I'd done it. I'd conquered the jerry-can carry.

I almost felt like I'd finished selection already. Almost.

*

Of course, there were still hurdles to cross. Those of us who were left – which was hardly anyone – were spaced out along a road with about five metres between each of us.

We were told that a truck was going to drive slowly down that road at some time in the next hour, and we had to be ready for it. The truck wasn't going to stop to pick us up – we would have to get our packs on, run and jump onto it. If you were asleep when it passed, too bad. Bye! You'd be heading back to your unit.

We sat there waiting, and we took turns on sentry, ten minutes at a time. We were all wasted, and sharing sentry meant we could get a bit of rest when it wasn't our turn, but we still had to be aware of what was going on. If you fell asleep, you'd be relying on the sentry to wake you up. Thankfully, I managed to stay awake and somehow I heard and chased that truck when it finally made its way down the road. My feet were wrecked and I could barely walk, but missing that truck was not an option.

I'm still here! I thought as soon as I made it onto the truck.

And, when the truck stopped, those of us who had made it onboard climbed down and were treated to a full breakfast. Our first proper meal in more than a week. It was even accompanied by a cup of tea and some water.

That was morale right there. It wasn't much – just a breakfast – but it gave us all a bit of hope.

*

Straight after breakfast, we were given our brief for the next two days: close-country navigation, which involved covering a similar distance to what we'd done in the open-country phrase but this time through the bush. The idea was that we had to cover the distance within a set timeframe – but we had to do it without getting caught by the roving patrols that would be driving up and down the roads the whole time. If one of them caught you, you'd be driven back down the road a few kilometres and have to re-cover that ground.

The easiest way to avoid getting caught was to stay off the roads and tracks by heading into the bush – but the *quickest* way to get to the destination was to stay *on* the roads and tracks. At the same time, the directing staff would take note if you used the road as a means to get to the end, and that alone could potentially get you booted from the course. This is where the 'who dares wins' attitude came in. If you didn't take risks, you wouldn't make it in time, but you had to be calculated about it.

We carried a ration pack with us from the start. There were a few reasons for this: it made our packs heavier, it would provide us with food in an emergency and, finally, it would test our discipline because we were not to go into it unless told to.

The exercise took place in the pine forest at Woodhill northwest of Auckland, and the roads there are long. You really had to have your wits about you. Whenever a V8 Rover was down the road, you could hardly hear it. You'd be walking along, and then all of a sudden you'd see it. The driver would put their foot down and you'd start running. At one point a group of us got pinged and ran, then all dropped down into the bush. I snuck into a clump of ferns. The patrol stopped alongside where we'd disappeared, and one of the badged members shouted, 'Right! Everyone, stand up!'

No, I thought. *I'm not getting up unless they actually see me.*

They got out of the Rover and started walking around, then one of them came and stood just across from where I was hiding. I tucked myself right into a fern bush ... but he saw me move. 'Get up!' he said.

I got up. There was no more room inside the Rover, so he made me sit on the bonnet where the spare wheel was. Then he took off back down the road. As we were driving, we caught two other guys who were on the road and just didn't have time to get off. They were shipped back a few kilometres, too.

When I got off the Rover, I ducked back into the bush and started making my way forward again. There wasn't one part of my body that didn't hurt. My hands were blistered, totally ripped to shreds, and every part of me ached. But I kept going. *This is just step one of the process*, I thought. *I want to be badged.*

Somehow, I managed to get to the final checkpoint within the cut-off time. Then I went to sleep.

*

The following morning we had to do a 60-kilometre route march down the road with full packs. There was no map, no watches. It was just, 'Walk that way and keep walking until we say stop.'

There were only 11 of us left by this stage. One by one, we walked off down the road and we kept walking ... and walking ... and walking. They kept us going deep into the night and it felt like it might never end – but I knew it would, eventually. And sooner rather than later. I was almost there. This was the final test. The end was so close. 'This is it,' I kept telling myself. 'All you have to do is keep walking down this road.'

After all the other tests, just walking down a road might sound easy. But I was utterly wrecked by this point, and the longer you go for the more it hurts, no matter what you're doing. Towards the end, my feet were so swollen I had to undo my laces, and I was just shuffling along the road, hallucinating, seeing people who weren't there. Then a bunch of guys who really *were* there suddenly turned up on quad bikes. They'd managed to get themselves lost. 'Do you know how to get out of the forest, man?' one of them said to me. I didn't even lift my head. I just said, 'Yeah nah, I've just got to keep going, mate,' and carried on shuffling. I don't know what they must have thought I was up to, but I'm pretty sure I would have looked like death.

Then I came up to another checkpoint.

'This is it,' the badged members waiting there said. 'You've done it.'

I couldn't believe it. I was an absolute shell of myself, and honestly I barely felt anything. I was just glad it was over.

I shuffled over to the truck, and finally took my pack off. It felt like it had been on my back forever. A support staff member put it on the truck, while I grabbed some fruit to eat and talked to the others who had made it. One of them was a guy called Rob, who I'd struck up a friendship with, and it was good to see he'd made it too. I was one of the last to arrive, so only had to wait an hour until we all got on the truck.

It was surreal. I'd never been that wrecked before, and in fact, I still haven't. I'd done it.

*

By the end of those nine days of selection, only 11 of us remained of the 70 who had started the course. But making it through selection was just Step One, the first part of the interview process.

We were put on a truck and taken back to base at Hobsonville and arrived at the barracks really late at night. There was no sleeping in the next morning: we had to be up at six in order to make sure we'd be ready by eight, when we'd get our final tick or flick.

Even after a full night's sleep, I could still hardly walk, my feet were so far gone. I couldn't help hobbling in pain when I was marched in to face the regimental CO, the training officer and the training sergeant major.

The CO was the first to speak. 'So, Jamie,' he said, 'how do you think you went on the selection course?'

'I think I did all right, sir.'

He nodded, then said, 'We'd like to accept you for further training. Would you like to carry on?'

'Yes, sir.'

'Good,' he replied. 'See you next year.'

And that was that. I'd got the tick.

I was totally physically, spiritually, mentally and emotionally drained, but I was also relieved. I'd gone out there to prove myself, and I'd done it. I had wanted to find out whether I could handle myself with the people I perceived to be 'the big dogs', and I'd shown myself I could.

It was the hardest thing I'd ever done at that point.

3

GETTING BADGED

MY NINE MONTHS OF intensive training towards becoming a badged member of the SAS kicked off with a two-week static-line parachuting course. Every SAS candidate on their cycle of post-selection training learns all the fundamental infiltration skills: parachuting, climbing, boating/amphibious and mobility. Then, you're selected to specialise in one of them. So, every SAS candidate learns static-line parachuting by day and night, then selected badged members will advance on to high-altitude freefall techniques.

Back in those days, we had a green-role squadron and a black-role squadron. The green role was all about bush skills and infiltration skills, while the black role focused on counterterrorism. There were about 28 of us at the start of the cycle, and we focused on green skills first. During this time, I knew I'd be under the microscope as an individual, but also as an individual within a team. It was at this point that team dynamics came into play. It was summer and it was hot, and we actually had a good time.

Rob, who I'd seen at the truck when I'd finally made it through selection, was there with us. He came onto our cycle as a patrol command from 2/1st Battalion, and was a very switched-on cookie. He helped to mentor us young fullas along the way, keeping us out of trouble, and he was very clear about right and wrong.

Another mate was there, too. Ricardo and I had been friends right since we'd begun our time in the unit together. We shared a sense of humour that most other people didn't get, and he also happened to be the most handsome chap among our cycle – something the other guys and I took advantage of, even if he didn't. The ladies would always flock to him at the bar, but he would just stand with his back to the corner and get drunk, then follow the rest of us out the door with his eyes closed and his groupies in tow. A very weird trait I have never seen anyone else replicate! Professionally, he was squared away and reliable. A genuine nice guy who would get amongst it once things kicked off. What you saw was what you got, and I respected that.

It was good to have these boys with me, and we became pretty close over time.

*

After the parachute training, we got into our basic courses. Combat lifesaving: basic medical training to deal with any kind of trauma – gunshot wounds, amputated limbs, bleeding, breathing, burns and breaks. Communication training: lots of radio work, and we also learnt to do Morse code in case we needed it for emergency comms. Heaps of skills-based stuff: live shooting, rappelling out of helicopters into trees, climbing natural features and so on.

And, finally, combat survival training in the Coromandel. It's now called Survive, Evade, Resist, Escape (SERE), because you learn how to employ all four of these words, as follows.

- Survive – develop the ability to survive over a number of weeks by making fire and shelter, and gathering water and food.
- Evade – understand and employ advanced evasion techniques against a technologically advantaged enemy force.
- Resist – resist enemy interrogation techniques.
- Escape – understand and employ escape techniques.

All things that you and/or your team will need to know if you're ever located by an enemy on the battlefield or overwhelmed by numbers and therefore have to cut and run. The 1993 book *Bravo Two Zero* by Andy McNab details a classic SERE example.

Prior to the course starting, we had to make our own clothes out of hessian, silk and plastic sheeting. We could make a jacket, gloves, a hat and a backpack. That was it. Our maps were drawn on silk, and we only had a button compass to navigate with. What's more, we weren't allowed watches; instead, we had to use the sun to tell the time. We got pretty good at it pretty quickly, but for some reason one of the boys decided he still needed a watch. So he smuggled one in by putting it up his butt. Yep. I still scratch my head over that one.

Then we got started with a week and a half of survival training. For the first two days, we were deliberately deprived of food so that we would experience what it was like to be properly hungry. The idea was to motivate us to really hunt for anything to eat. Then we spent a couple of days negotiating a mini 'evade' exercise, before being picked up by trucks and 'put in the bag' to be interrogated.

First, we were blindfolded and given overalls to wear – the big guys got really small overalls, and the smaller guys really baggy ones. Then, we spent 12 hours being interrogated. They'll try anything to get you to talk. In one room, you might get an interrogator who's in your face, berating you, while in another room you're given food and your interrogator is really nice, saying things like, 'We're from the Red Cross. What's going on? Tell me your circumstances.' Others are equally gentle, promising, 'We'll get you out of here if you just sign this bit of paper.'

To pass interrogation, you can only provide certain limited information, and you've just got to stick to it no matter what they try. If you go off-script and start talking about something else, you've failed. That shows you'll speak when you're under pressure. It also puts you at risk. The longer you don't give them any information, the more frustrated they can get. They'd often turn. They'd take the food you refused away and start saying, 'You're not going to get any food then!'

After the interrogation was done, we were walked outside, still blindfolded and also wearing earmuffs. Then we were suddenly forced to stop, and our blindfolds were ripped off. The bright daylight was a shock, and as my eyes adjusted I realised I was standing on the edge of what looked like a cliff. At the same moment I looked down I felt a hand push my back, and I fell. My heartrate shot up. I had no idea how far the drop was ...

It turned out to only be three or four metres. I landed in a stream, but before I could get my bearings, my head was pushed underwater, then pulled up again, and then I was chucked out of the water and told to get in line.

It was a difficult course and a steep learning curve across a number of different areas. Once the whole thing was finished, we had to pack up the camp, then it was back on the trucks to Waiouru.

*

By this time, we were a few months into our training, and the season had noticeably changed. We'd started in summer, and now it was the beginning of winter – and this change was made even more noticeable when we headed from the Coromandel south to Tūrangi.

From there, we were tasked with making our own way to Waiouru. By road, that's a trip along the Desert Road of just over 60 kilometres, but we had to take the long way around. Our route would cover around 100 kilometres – and we'd have people chasing us. The police and their dogs plus a whole company, to be specific – with assets including tracked vehicles and helicopters, and technology including night-vision goggles (NVGs) and maybe even thermal-imaging capability.

The landscape on the Desert Road is bleak and lacking in natural cover, and in winter it's frigidly cold. Out there in our handmade clothes with a handful of dried goat meat to last who knew how long, we had to go from checkpoint to checkpoint within a set timeframe. We wore only the basic clothes we'd made during our survival training plus our army trousers and boots, and some gloves that looked and felt like oven mitts. On our backs were small packs containing the small bag of dried goat meat we'd made on survival training, a tin we could use as a cooking vessel and some water-purifying tablets. We had no raincoats or wet-weather gear. If we were lucky, we might get some more food at each checkpoint – perhaps an onion, half a cabbage or a couple of potatoes – but it was still barely enough to sustain us as we raced around the Central Plateau trying to avoid capture.

Working together as a group, we decided to try to cover as many kilometres as we could the first night, while we still had a bit of energy. We managed to get quite a long way. The following morning, we woke up to heavy rain. Some of the guys went out to find out where the next checkpoint was, and when they came back they told us that one of the guys had decided he didn't want to go any further, so that was him gone. We stayed put for the day and slept under a big tarpaulin sheet.

That night, the rain subsided and it was really foggy, so we decided to take a bit of risk by moving along the road. Visibility was down to about a metre, and our plan if someone was close to getting to us was to just stay and fight. We were walking up the road with some big sticks we'd picked up along the way when Ricardo stopped and quietly said, 'I think I hear something.'

We got off the road and sat silently for a while. All was quiet, so we started creeping forward up the road again. All of a sudden, we were caught in the beam of a Unimog's lights and a voice bellowed, 'Hold there!'

One of the guys dropped immediately to the ground. The rest of us threw our sticks in the direction of the light, then we just broke off and started running. We could hear the Mog chasing us, and we just kept running up ahead of it in a line, when – *oof!* We suddenly dropped out of sight. Literally.

We'd fallen into what appeared to be a below-ground stream. Above us, we could see the slit we'd tumbled through, and it was covered over by tussock. Every now and then, torch beams flashed overhead as our pursuers walked around, trying to figure out where we'd got to. About 200 metres away, we could see another way out, so we inched our way towards it and back out to freedom.

We could barely believe our luck. If we'd been caught, they'd have interrogated us then dropped us back out in the middle of nowhere with a warning not to get caught again or we'd find ourselves heading back to battalion.

As for the guy who went down instead of running? We met up with him at a rendezvous point two days later, and learnt he'd managed to ninja his way out of getting caught. He'd then spent the rest of the time out there by himself.

*

Finally, we made it to the last rendezvous point. There, we got on the truck. We'd made it to the finish without being captured, but we weren't quite done yet.

The Unimog set off. We were right at the back of it, and the flap was down, so we had no idea where we were, but they seemed to be taking us for a bit of a tiki tour. Then all of a sudden, the truck came to a stop. 'Get out of the truck now,' we heard someone command. A head popped into sight under the flap, and disappeared again. 'Get out now!'

So the first guy did as instructed – but the moment he got out, someone grabbed him. They'd made a ring around the truck so we *couldn't* get out. We saw the first guy fighting his captors, and we all jumped off and started to fight these guys. Then they let the dogs loose on us, and one guy got bitten on the leg (something that would never happen nowadays). He started yelling in pain, and that was when we all went to ground. They put hoods and earmuffs on us, then loaded us back onto the truck.

From that point on, we were treated as if we were prisoners of war. They drove us to a camp, and when we got there they put us through the interrogation process again. We still had no idea where we were, and again the interrogation lasted 12 hours. This time they had a platoon of visiting Fijian soldiers as the guard force. Back on the Coromandel, the guard force had been badged guys, and you could tell the difference between the badged guys and the non-badged ones. They were all hard, but the badged guys were that bit harder. They were just ruthless, especially when we were put in stress positions. If my arms came off my head, they'd grab my hands and slam them back in place. They'd put their knee in my back to make it straighter, then they'd stand there and wait for me to collapse again. It was pretty brutal.

I was very relieved when it came to an end and I made it through.

*

Our next course was patrol procedures. This takes six weeks, and it is central to how the SAS does business – the tactics, techniques and procedures you learn apply across all other regiment capabilities. The crux of it is the live-firing phase, during which you're tested on your ability to shoot, move, communicate and medicate in close proximity with other people in a bush environment. It requires really good comms, weapon handling, situational awareness and plugging gaps.

In the middle of the patrol-procedures course, they basically cut our whole group in half. One of the directing staff called out a list of names, including mine, then said, 'OK, you guys jump on this truck.' It was a nervous moment. Was I being sent back to Auckland? But on the truck I looked around and relaxed. With me were Rob, Ricardo and another guy called Roo. These guys were on to it. *I'm pretty sure I'm staying*, I thought.

And, by the time we got back from the rest of our training that day, the guys we'd left behind were already on their way back to their units. It must have been gutting to make it that far only to be sent packing.

It was ruthless, but it also gave me confidence. I'd survived the selection course, and I'd managed to keep myself in training so far. Now, it was down to just a core group of soldiers – and I was one of them.

*

We finished the patrol-procedures course with a long patrol. It's a key part of the cycle of training, and incorporates everything you have been taught up to that point. It's a confirmation of your ability to operate in a small patrol, and a couple more people got taken off the course after it.

That brought us to the end of the green-skills phase, so it was on to black skills: counterterrorism training. The purpose of this phase is to develop the individual and collective skills needed to effectively carry out counterterrorist operations. This is important because NZSAS is responsible for resolving terrorist events either nationally or regionally.

As a group, we were divided into marksmen and assaulters. Along with Ricardo, Rob and Roo, I was assigned to the marksmen group, and our task was essentially to report back information about the Alpha, or target, area. During the assault phase, we also provided precision fires. There's a long-standing piss-take that marksmen are selected because they have a higher level of intelligence and are better at shooting than those selected as assaulters. Which I'm obviously going to tell you is true, but no one wants to acknowledge it.

After that, we did a basic unarmed combat course. We each had two fights every day, no gloves or anything – it was all elbows and open-palm strikes. On the last day of that course, we had to show we knew what we were doing in all sorts of scenarios, including disarming people with knives, pistols, bats and other weapons. And then we had another couple of fights with our classmates. All this fighting inevitably resulted in people getting cut open or having their noses broken. It was brutal, but necessary.

*

Each squadron in the regiment is divided into four troops, and each troop specialises in a different area: mobility, amphibious, air or mountain operations. We had to do basic skills courses in each specialisation, and our cycle would then be assigned to either Mountain Troop or Air Troop, depending on how we did.

I did pretty well in the basic climbing course, but what I really wanted was to be in the Air Troop, because that's where they do all the parachuting! I already enjoyed sky-diving out of a Cessna going at 50 knots, but that didn't compare to jumping out of a Hercules going at 120 knots. Thankfully, I got picked for the Air Troop – and that meant I got to do the Military Freefall (MFF) course up at Whenuapai, which involved skydiving, HALO (high-altitude, low-opening) jumps and HAHO (high-altitude, high-opening) jumps.

The MFF course is an advanced parachuting course designed to develop the skills needed to infiltrate a specified area at night out of a C-130 with weapons, equipment and people. This is something that is achieved with very low jump numbers, and is well outside the scope of civilian parachuting operations. Sorties are conducted as both individuals and teams, depending on the training requirements. During team training jumps, all parachutists locate each other in freefall and stay in a group until opening. These jumps were the riskiest – but also the most rewarding and fun when done well.

*

Throughout the entire cycle of SAS training, it was never a given that we'd make it to badging. All the time, guys were being dropped. It wasn't until we got to the last course, infiltration, that we were pretty sure we'd made it all the way. Then, it was a case of 'go have some fun'. We did a couple of days of option training, learning how to operate and do assaults in high-rise buildings, trains, planes and other types of urban targets. And, on our final day of the cycle of training, we were out flying around Auckland in helicopters, integrating with the badged members, until five in the morning.

We got back to base, and immediately turned our attention to getting scrubbed up. There was no time for sleep because our badging ceremony was starting in four hours' time.

Former All Black captain Sir Wilson Whineray was the colonel commandant who handed us our sand berets that Friday morning in October 1998. Of the original 28 men who'd been on the course at the beginning of the year, only 11 of us had made it to the end.

It was an incredibly proud moment for all of us.

We had each earnt the right to wear our berets and the regiment's blue staple belt. While others had dropped off through first the selection course and then the cycle of training, we had remained. We were still here. We deserved to be here.

For me, the moment was made especially meaningful by having Mum there to see it. I'd achieved this huge goal, but without her wise advice to go for the thing I really wanted I might never have got on that bus to Waiouru.

Getting that beret was a big deal, but it didn't give any of us permission to rest on our laurels. There's a saying: 'It's harder to keep it than to earn it.' This was just the beginning. It felt great to have made it into the SAS, but I knew that I was going to have to keep working hard to stay there. I still had to put my hand up for everything and anything.

This was when the real journey started. From then on, I would have to maintain that pace and tempo for my whole career.

4

WE ARE THE PILGRIMS

THERE WAS A REAL sense of brotherhood in the regiment. We knew that we could do things individually, but it was easier for us to do them collectively. I could look into the eyes of every single man who'd been badged and know that we had all been through the same gates. There was no doubt who any of them were. I knew that they could all be trusted.

Even so, we were tested every single day. There was no room for backing off, for taking your foot off the pedal or hiding from responsibility. As new guys, we all did a two-year probation, during which time we were watched to make sure we demonstrated the culture and kept up the tempo. You couldn't come off that gruelling cycle of training and think, *I'm in the squadron now, so I can just chill out.* That's not what it was about. Once you were in, you were expected to go harder. Then for each rank level you took on, it got harder again, because you'd be taking on more responsibility.

From very early on, we had the following words from a poem called *The Golden Road to Samarkand* instilled in us.

> We are the Pilgrims, master; we shall go
> Always a little further; it may be
> Beyond that last blue mountain barred with snow
> Across that angry or that glimmering sea,
>
> White on a throne or guarded in a cave
> There lies a prophet who can understand
> Why men were born: but surely we are brave,
> Who take the Golden Road to Samarkand.

That poem was written by British poet James Elroy Flecker and originally published in 1913. It's really significant to the regiment, and served as a reminder to us that, no matter what was thrown at us, we always had to try to go that bit further. No matter what obstacles we might encounter along the way. It was just one foot in front of the other, like the pilgrim on his journey.

*

I'd been in the regiment just under a year when word started to get around that a deployment to East Timor might be on the cards. The United Nations had requested support following an independence referendum held there in August 1999.

Like all of the boys, I was keen to get out there and put the skills I'd learnt and trained for over the past two years into action. And, sure enough, a squadron was deployed – but it was A Squadron. They left really quickly and without a definitive end date to their deployment. Meanwhile, I stayed at home with the rest of B Squadron. Our job? To be on stand-by to respond to any significant security incident at the Asia-Pacific Economic Cooperation (APEC) summit taking place in Auckland. Keeping an eye on international leaders like Bill Clinton and the Sultan of Brunei was all good, but I would rather have been on the ground in Timor. I'd wanted to join the SAS so I could go on operations, and when I saw A Squadron head off I just felt gutted to not be going with them. I was still a young fella, and I couldn't see the bigger picture yet.

So, feeling like I was stuck here in New Zealand, I cast my mind a bit further afield ... and decided I was going to have a crack at joining the British SAS. It wasn't common for guys to do this, but it did happen often enough that there were unofficial rules around it. One was that the officer commanding (OC) thought it was better if you did three years in the regiment before going to England. This thinking, whether right or wrong, came from a good place: you'd be flying the flag for New Zealand over in the UK, and they wanted to make sure you'd represent the unit well and uphold the reputation of the regiment.

My thinking was a bit different. I'd done selection, I'd been badged, I was in the squadron, and I knew I'd be competing in the UK with people who weren't even badged. So why would I need to spend another three years before going? So, still being young and wanting to have an adventure, I left B Squadron and headed over to England to do my version of an OE.

*

I made it all the way through to the jungle phase of the British SAS selection course before I had to stop and take stock of what I was doing. We'd been flown from Oxfordshire out to Brunei, where we were based near Tutong. By this point in selection, guys were dropping like flies – the helicopter would be in multiple times a day to collect people as they dropped out or got cut. At the end of the first week, we'd gone from 100 to about 30.

It was brutal, but it all made sense. It was all about mimicking going out on operations. You might be in England one moment, but the next you could find yourself in the jungle, and you had to be able to operate in either environment. After the jungle phase, they knew they'd be left with a group of guys able to handle whatever was thrown at them, able to operate straight away in any environment. I desperately wanted to be one of those guys.

But it was at this point that I was forced to do some soul searching. Back home, I'd been having money issues, and it was becoming clear I needed to get things sorted. Money was the last thing I wanted to have to think about while I was in the jungle in Brunei, but there was no avoiding it. I made the call to drop out and go home.

It was a really tough decision, especially when I'd got so close to finishing the jungle phase, but I knew it was the right thing to do. I believe it happened for a reason, and I don't have any regrets.

*

Deciding to come home left me with a whole lot of other decisions to make. I had a house, but I needed a job.

I met up with some of the boys to talk about my plans, and said I was thinking about seeing if I could come back to the regiment.

One guy raised his eyebrows. 'You'd have to talk to the OC about that ...'

Everyone knew I hadn't had a great relationship with my OC before leaving. To be honest, that was down to my maturity level. He'd taken a bit of a dislike to me, and so he should have!

'Yeah, I don't think I'll ring him first,' I said.

'He's the last person you want to ring!' my mate said.

And, as it turns out, he *was* the last person I rang. No one else would answer my calls.

'What do you want?' he asked gruffly when he realised it was me.

'I've come back from England,' I replied.

'Oh, yeah. Is that right? And what are you going to do?'

'Well, I was wondering if I could come back …'

'We'll see about that.'

And that was the end of the conversation.

*

Despite the chilly reception, I did get called in for an interview with two senior members of the regiment. One, named Peter, sat close by and stared pointedly at the side of my head, while the other quizzed me on the hows and whys of me ending up back there. He was a training officer, and also very well respected. We called him the Oracle because he'd been around for decades and had a tonne of operational knowledge.

'OK, we'll take all of that into consideration,' he said, once I'd finished explaining myself. 'But the decision has actually already been made. You've got two options. One: you can go down to battalion for a year, then we'll consider whether or not we should bring you back.'

I wasn't thrilled at this idea, but then he added, 'Two: we make you do selection again.'

My reaction must have been a bit more obvious than I meant for it to be.

'But that does seem a bit ridiculous, seeing as you've just come off selection,' the Oracle said.

The reasoning behind sending me back into regular forces, he explained, was to give me the opportunity to show I was serious about wanting to rejoin the regiment. The way I'd left things, especially with the relationship breakdown between me and my OC, didn't exactly count in my favour. 'Go down there, do your time and do it well,' the Oracle said. 'And then we'll consider whether we want you to come back or not.'

It was a real lesson in humility, and probably one of the best things that ever happened to me.

*

I hadn't had much to do with Peter before then, but a day later he rang me up and asked if I wanted to come round to his house that Saturday to talk about things. By that point, I wasn't really even contemplating going back. I'd decided to do something else. Join the police maybe. But I went round anyway.

'So, tell me what you're thinking,' he said.

'I really don't want to go back to battalion,' I said. 'And I understand that I was at least partly responsible for the way things were with my OC, but every relationship is a two-way street. So, honestly? I feel like I might as well get out and do something else.'

'Hold your horses,' he said. 'Did you know that your battalion is going to Timor next year? If you want to go on operations, then this is your chance. Don't discount going back to battalion. You've got to think about these things.'

'Yeah, I don't know ...' I said.

'Look, just take the kick in the arse,' he said. 'Go down for a year, go away on operations and come back. It's going to be easy, anyway. You might as well.'

I thought about it, and I had to admit he was right. He'd managed to change my mind.

As I was leaving, he put his hand on my shoulder. 'Hey, don't tell anyone that you and I had this discussion,' he said. 'It's just between you and me.'

Up until that point, I'd seen those of us in the regiment as quite a black-and-white bunch of people. If you crossed the line and violated the values of the regiment, it was a cardinal sin, and therefore you had leave. There was nothing in between. That was what I believed – but our conversation that day showed me I was mistaken. Just because that's how I saw things, that didn't mean that's how they were.

Peter saw things differently. He didn't have to open up his home to me that day. We could have just as easily had that talk over the phone, but for whatever reason he decided we needed to do it in person. Maybe he understood how stubborn I can be – once I make a decision, I tend to go with it no matter what – and he knew that would be the only way to change my mind. Whatever the case, he obviously saw something in me that I didn't see at the time.

Over the years, I've reflected on that conversation many times. Whenever I've found myself having similar conversations with people who have decided they're going to go wayward, I've urged them – like Peter did for me – to learn the lesson. I believe that obstacles get put in your way for a reason. You might get around one or two, but the same thing is going to keep getting put in front of you in different ways until you work through it.

I'm a spiritual guy by nature, and I believe things like that happen for a reason. If I hadn't gone to see Peter that day, my life would have taken a very different path. He helped me to course correct, and I'm forever grateful.

*

So I took the knock, went back down to battalion, shut my mouth and got on with things. And, six months later, I was on my way to East Timor with the 1st Battalion, Royal New Zealand Infantry Regiment (RNZIR).

New Zealand and Australia were the main forces in East Timor at the time. UK's special forces maritime unit, the

Special Boat Service (SBS) came down and the Irish Rangers were there as well, so there was a strong special forces presence. We were operating as part of the United Nations Transitional Authority East Timor (UNTAET).

I was in Suai, in the Immediate Reaction Force, a platoon supporting the regiment and other New Zealand sub units across East Timor. Right next door to us lived the NZSAS tracking patrol, which three of my cycle-mates were part of. It was a strange feeling to be on the outside.

Acting on sightings of militia or reported incidents, our job was to follow in behind the NZSAS trackers. If they got contacted, we had to get in front of them and start assaulting – or, if we were close enough, close with the enemy force and try to kill or capture them. I also deployed with Recon Platoon when they required additional patrol members, spending sometimes up to nine days conducting observation posts at strategic points, but it was actually pretty uneventful. There were things that happened in the area of operations, like a shoot-up with a guy in a riverbed, but I wasn't involved with anything like that. About the most exciting it got was running into an Indonesian patrol on one of our walks up the border, but other than that it was really just an exercise in intensive and regular patrolling.

After three months in Suai, we went up to Junction Point Echo at Belulik Leten, about 50 kilometres inland and

10 kilometres from the Indonesian border. We had a forward operating base there that we choppered in and out of, and I spent another few months there.

Then it was back home to Linton, where I finished up my year back in the battalion and awaited the verdict of the SAS commanders. And, thankfully, they decided to let me return to the regiment.

*

By the time I got back to Hobsonville, one squadron of the regiment had already left to serve in Afghanistan, and another was getting ready to replace them. They were there as part of Operation Concord, which was part of Operation Enduring Freedom, and joined up with forces from the US, Canada, Germany, Norway, Denmark and Turkey to become Task Force K-Bar. This had all been initiated by the United States government in response to the 9/11 attacks, and fed into what became known as the global war on terror.

The squadron deployed on 11 December 2001, and was tasked with reconnaissance work and sensitive site exploration. Much of this was done on foot, with helicopter support, and each deployment was to last for three months.

When the time came for a third rotation to go to the country, everyone was called into a meeting. 'We're going to call out the names of everyone who's going on the next trip to

Afghanistan,' they said. One by one, the Oracle called out the name of every single person in the room but one: mine.

I sat there feeling absolutely deflated. I couldn't believe it! I'd just done a year back at battalion, I'd been to Timor, I'd got good reports, and now this? I got up and walked straight out of the meeting. *Stuff this*, I thought. Once again I was ready to get out and go join the police.

I was sitting in my room in the barracks when one of the guys knocked on my door. 'The Oracle wants to see you,' he said.

So I got up and walked back to where the meeting had been held.

'Where did you go?' he asked.

'Back to the barracks,' I replied.

'Why?'

'I was pissed off that I didn't get picked.'

'Yeah, I could see that,' he said. 'Pretty hard to miss with your bottom lip dragging on the ground like that.' Then he laughed.

I was confused. This wasn't funny.

'You're going,' the Oracle said.

'I am?'

'You are.'

He laughed again, and I smiled at last. It was that humour and humility the regiment prized so highly. They were just keeping me in my place.

5

AFGHANISTAN

FLYING TO AFGHANISTAN WAS an expedition in its own right. The New Zealand Air Force Hercules only have a range of about 4,000 kilometres, so on our trip from Auckland we had to stop in Australia, then Malaysia, then Diego Garcia – an island in the Indian Ocean that houses a US base – then Dubai, where we stayed a couple of days to get the humming of the Herc out of our heads. Then it was back in the air all the way to Kandahar, in southern Afghanistan, where we'd be based.

When the original Kiwi contingent first arrived at this base back in 2001, it had only just been cleared of Taliban forces by US troops. By the time we arrived, it was made up of a selection of bombed-out buildings and damaged infrastructure and had been improved a bit, but it wasn't anything like the bases we'd stopped at on our long trip. There were five or six accommodation buildings, but one was bombed out and roped off, and there was a large parking area for the Humvees and another little block with showers. We had a small operations room, another room for our support crew, and something that no one else in camp had: a nice green lawn area, which we kept well watered. Other than that, though, it was fairly bare-bones.

In some ways it was pretty fitting, as we didn't bring much to the table in terms of hardware, either. There had been no operational deployment between Vietnam in 1971 and Kuwait in 1998, and the New Zealand Government's investment in the regiment had dropped off in the years since. They didn't really know what the regiment was capable of. But the US president at the time, George W. Bush, only wanted special forces to do the work in Afghanistan, and it was when we were deployed there that our own government started to see the boost we could give to New Zealand's international reputation. That was when a bit more money started to come in.

When the regiment first got to Kandahar, they had no vehicles. The first rotation conducted traditional Special Reconnaissance work, but the second rotation did mobility for half of our time there. Having no vehicles made life pretty difficult, given we were tasked with long-range reconnaissance missions. So, a few of the boys went down to the spot where all the Americans' Humvees were parked, and asked, 'How do you get those vehicles?'

'Talk to my boss,' was the reply.

'We've got some whiskey and some beers ...'

'How much?'

They managed to get eight desert Humvees for four bottles of whiskey and some trays of Lion Red. The American bases were dry, so as well as being open to this sort of trade, they enjoyed coming over to ours for a cold beer from time to time.

Our 'social functions' really helped us to grease the wheels and get whatever we needed. We had the Canadian Joint Task Force 2 guys (the Canadian Armed Forces' special operations force) next door, and we developed a really good partnership with them. Relationships and engagements are key to the success of an operation, so we would invite anyone and everyone we thought might be able to help us to the parties at our camp. It was amazing how much leverage we got out of pouring cans of Lion Red! Beer proved to be a very popular currency.

Back then, Kandahar airfield was pretty basic, but we had a benefactor in New Zealand who would send us 'welfare packages'. They would get flown into base for us, and included things like TVs, DVD players and DVD movies, and always a pallet of precious beer. Uzbekistan vodka, which cost about 60 cents a bottle, also used to find its way to the base at Kandahar. The Uzbeki supply runs also meant that we often got fresh food.

We had to do our own food, and our cook did the best he could with what we had: big tins of preserved meat, maybe some creamed rice, whatever fresh food we could get. Stuff like that. It all got put into bain maries and served up so we *felt* like we were in a mess, but we were really just eating ration packs in bulk. Over the years, things improved a bit, though, and we got mess tents and even a shop where you could buy food.

Since we were under-resourced, we often had to do the typical Kiwi thing and make do with what we had. This was way back in the day when things like weapons mounts were only just starting to be manufactured. We didn't have the luxury of sitting around waiting for things like that to arrive. The only way we were going to get them was if we made them ourselves. So we'd go out to the dump and get things like bed frames, then cut them down to make rudimentary mounts. They were very effective. Not great at range, but they did the trick. We had proper mounts for the main weapon, but we made our own for everything else.

We also got hold of some big plywood boxes, which we stuck on the back of our vehicles, and we'd put all our ration packs, onions, potatoes and cookware in them. It was a glamping-worthy set-up. So good in fact that Delta Force came out, took photos of those boxes and started replicating them on their vehicles! That was something that happened periodically throughout our tours: the Americans would get sent out to see what the Kiwis were doing, because we were always doing something a bit different.

*

When Western forces went into Afghanistan in 2001, their initial focus had been to overthrow the Taliban with the goal of establishing a democratic Afghan government. After that, special forces were relied on to secure airfields and to carry out counterterrorist operations in order to help bring about a greater sense of security across the country.

To play our part in that process, we were sent out on long-range patrols to gather information about what was happening out in the harder-to-reach parts of the country. To begin with, those patrols were done on foot, but in May 2002 the regiment shifted to mounted operations. Those Humvees acquired from our friends allowed the patrols to move further faster, and were accompanied by outriders on motorbikes, who provided extra security. True to our tight budgets, we had Kawasaki 250s. They're trail bikes, but they're the sort of bike you'd expect to see on the farm. That was all the army had. They were painted in desert colours, but that was the only real modification made to them.

These patrols were expected to cover 2,000 kilometres or more, and would be away from the base for up to 30 days at a time. The goal was to look for the rough edges – places where attacks were likely to occur, or anywhere that might serve as an airfield or forward operating base – and also to gather intelligence and gain an understanding of what the general political feeling was out in the provinces. Before we were even on the ground, we were always briefed into the situation. That brief included the landscape of the local area, who was in it, who we needed to look out for and how we needed to conduct ourselves. We had to understand who the big players were before we engaged with anyone. As a young soldier, I took that on board, but really, we all relied on the Troop Commander and the Troop Sergeant to take care of that sort of stuff, because they were the ones interfacing.

When our deployment arrived in Kandahar, the previous one was still in camp. They took us though an induction process, and then we all went out on operations together. Our warm-up patrols together were in the mountainous parts of central Afghanistan. This was home to the Hazara people, who were generally friendly to coalition forces and visitors. Those patrols were just fact-finding missions to help us get our feet on the ground before we got pushed out further. They were a good chance to get our standard operating procedures sorted, and to familiarise ourselves with the vehicles – we didn't have Humvees back in New Zealand.

Once the other squadron returned to New Zealand, though, we started moving into bandit country. These areas were generally run by the Pashtun people, and the difference between them and the Hazara was night and day. As well as looking for Taliban and areas of interest, we were also on the hunt for caves, because they were often used to hide weapons, ammunition and equipment. There, we drove around keeping an eye out, and acting on intelligence we gained. If someone said, 'The Taliban are over here,' or, 'There's a weapons cache over there,' we'd look into it.

It was pretty hard to know who was Taliban and who wasn't. There was a huge amount of raw opium and money being transported around the country, and everyone had AK-47s. We'd stop vehicles full of armed guys, money and raw opium. They'd ask us what we wanted, and when we said that we were going to search their vehicles, they'd let us do it. They didn't present a threat because we didn't either. We didn't have a mandate to do anything about the raw opium. We knew it was being transported to drug-production sites in country, where it was converted into opiates or possibly heroin, then transported to the borders and sold on for huge amounts money, but we had to just let them go on their way.

This sort of long-range reconnaissance brought with it a lot of risk. We went deep into Afghanistan, where warlords were running around the countryside. We were as far from support as it was possible to be, and we were out there by ourselves. So, within each troop, we were self-sufficient and had all the skills and equipment – including medics and advanced comms people – that we needed to conduct a range of mission sets if required.

The countryside was epic. As far as the eye could see, there were just mountains, scree and desert. At night, you could see every single star in the sky. I saw shooting stars all the time. Some nights, it was so bright that the stars almost illuminated the ground without the light of the moon. I'd just sit there, stare up at the sky, and watch the shooting stars going down while the wolves howled.

*

We ended up heading out on a four-week long-range patrol, and flew out of Kandahar at night on four MC-130H Talon IIs, which are like Hercules C-130s on steroids, with two vehicles on each aircraft, plus motorbikes. Our destination was an airfield in Herat province in northwest Afghanistan, over 100 kilometres from the Iranian border to the west and the border with Turkmenistan to the north. Home to nearly four million people, Herat is the second-most populated province in the country after Kabul, with most of its people speaking Persian rather than Pashtun.

We flew into an airfield to the south of Herat 30 seconds later than was anticipated, according to our Talon's apologetic loadmaster. The airfield was secured by the Afghan National Army (ANA), and on arrival we liaised with a US special forces group who drove us to our infiltration start point off the main road heading north towards the city. Our American escort then headed to Herat, where they had the closest forward operating base to us.

As for us, we started driving up the highway, and on command turned off our lights and switched to NVGs, before turning off the road and driving into the darkness. Our area of operation was further south, and we wanted to reach it undetected. I was one of two motorcycle outriders, and we earnt our money on those things – it was hard work. Our job, depending on the terrain, was to stay a couple of kilometres ahead of the rest of the troop, route-finding and providing early warning of any threats ahead. If we got shot at, we'd turn round and move at speed to get back to the main convoy. Our main goal was to keep the convoy moving. We worked our arses off, trying to get up onto high features and gain a bit of visibility and see ahead. It was a real challenge getting the bikes up some of the hills, and we had to zig-zag all the way, with the Kawasakis' motors absolutely screaming. We'd end up doing about three times the distance that the convoy did, so at the end of the day we were absolutely wrecked – and the days were about 16 hours long. And that was on a good day! Sometimes, we'd end up doing 36 hours straight in the saddle. In terms of enduro-riding, you can't top that. I got so good at riding that I could go anywhere.

We avoided villages if we could, and went underground in dry river channels called wadis during the day to keep below ground and out of sight. We'd try to sleep, but it was difficult because it was still so hot. Then we'd do all of our driving at night. Occasionally, we would stop in at villages to talk to the leaders and see if we could glean any information about the Taliban, or any weapons or ammunition caches. 'We'll be just down the road for the next couple of hours,' we'd explain through our interpreter. 'Come and find us if you have anything you want to tell us.'

The Oracle was the ground commander, and just watching him operate gave me the blueprint for how to do business. As well as being incredibly experienced, he also had an innate understanding of diplomacy. He was very good at reading the terrain and understanding exactly what was needed. Whenever he met governors or the head men of a village, he just knew what to do and how to talk. If he was about to shake hands with someone, he'd always take his glove off first as a sign of respect. He was also big on making sure to look the person in the eyes as he shook their hand. He'd share his smokes and drink chai. Gifts are also quite an important part of Afghan culture, so he always made sure we had the appropriate small things to give people when we met. Not many people would think to do those sorts of things, but it was what opened doors for us when we needed protection.

Despite our best efforts, though, the people in some areas were completely opposed to us being there; really hostile. Sometimes, we got attacked because they thought we were working with their rival warlords. Then we'd have to figure out who these people were, and go out to get the truth on the ground. We were able to do it because we travelled in small groups, and had plenty of fire power and punch, and we were good at it because we knew how to connect with people on a hearts and minds basis.

Don't get me wrong. We didn't take any shit, but we did always put in the time to figure out what was going on before we jumped to action. Coming from New Zealand, we just couldn't know what it was like to be oppressed by a group that is pretty much a gang going around doing whatever it wants. The people we met who were under Taliban rule weren't free – they all had to watch themselves, because they were being watched.

It was important to us to do the right thing by the local people. We always made sure we were visible and away from villages, so that if anything happened it wasn't right in the middle of a built-up area. That way, we could keep everyone safe. Whenever we were invited into a village, we'd be given the best meals – goat curries and bread and Zamzam, which is the Iranian version of Coca-Cola.

Our approach as Kiwis was a bit different from that of some of the other countries with forces there. We knew that the best thing to do was to go in with smiles on our faces, greeting everyone and being open to meeting them. Some of the Māori boys in the regiment, in particular, connected with the tribal aspect of the Afghani people, and that gave them a link to the community. Even being able to say we were from New Zealand was a conversation starter, because hardly anyone had any idea where that was.

All that really set us apart. We were good at doing simple things, and that made a difference. For us, making friends with people made our job easier. Some other forces didn't have any of that. They were there to do a job, and didn't seem to care about anything else. And, to some, that job was to simply destroy the enemy – even if it wasn't always clear who that enemy was. They saw things as very black and white, and didn't stop to consider the impact of their actions on people who might not be combatants.

*

As we headed further south in Herat, we found ourselves crossing from the territory of one warlord into that of another. There was a demarcation line between their two territories, and we had to carefully negotiate our way through it. To do that, we made our way around off-road.

One night, though, we had no choice but to drive through a village. It was right next to a riverbed, and the valley was so steep-sided that there was no way round. Not far from the village, we could see AK-47 tracer fire going up into the air. Then we saw another line of tracer going up, so we knew our presence had been detected and was being signalled.

The pair of us on motorbikes got out of the village, and headed up and away from the convoy. We had infra-red strobes blinking on and off for the convoy to follow, and when we were about a kilometre up the road, we turned our bikes off and stopped to watch the convoy come in.

Boom! Boom! Boom! Boom!

The sound came from quite a heavy machine gun, and it was somewhere to my left. I radioed the patrol: 'Shots fired to the east.'

Then, all of a sudden, all these rounds came straight over the top of us, and exploded a couple of metres over our heads.

I radioed again: 'I think they're firing at us!'

We jumped back on our bikes, spun round and took off. As soon as we started riding, the shooters upped their rate of fire in an attempt to get us off our bikes. They cracked off another couple of rounds before I realised the fire was coming from an anti-aircraft gun. They were perfectly on for line, but their elevation was just off. We found out later that they'd mounted two anti-aircraft guns on a wall, and the only reason they couldn't get the elevation on us was that they couldn't pitch the guns low enough to get us. That was the only thing that saved us. If they'd had the elevation right, they'd have knocked us off our bikes and we'd have been killed.

Pedal to the metal, we approached the convoy, bringing the enemy rounds with us. When the convoy registered that we were being shot at, they turned their guns in the direction of the anti-aircraft fire. We were on.

When the shooters turned their fire on the convoy, they still couldn't get the gun low enough. So we just sat there and laid volume on them. I decided to get amongst it by firing my rifle, but that was doing absolutely nothing. It had a maximum effectiveness of about 600 metres, and these guys were at least a kilometre away. There were a couple of American special tactics guys riding with us, and one of them was on a 40-millimetre grenade launcher. He wasn't that capable with it, but he was firing away anyway.

Then I saw explosions impacting on the ground in front of us, and an illumination round appeared to our left.

'I think we're being mortared!' I said to the vehicle commander next to me.

The message was relayed to the Oracle, who commanded the troop to break right and get out of there. That was when some guys from the village decided to jump out, firing at us from the rear. As we were possibly taking incoming mortars, this wasn't something that we wanted to play with, so we stopped firing in front of us and peeled out. Breaking right, we took off into the darkness.

Once we were sufficiently far away, we regrouped, then drove off into the night. We eventually located a piece of ground that afforded us a good defensive position, and stopped there, but we stayed on high alert the rest of the night.

Later, I found out that the joint terminal attack controller (JTAC) attached to our troop had asked the Oracle if he wanted to call in an airstrike. A JTAC essentially vectors in Close Air Support to conduct airstrikes. Aircraft are always up in theatre, and there are different types to choose from depending on your needs.

The Oracle refused, stating there would be too much collateral damage. Bombing support would likely have resulted in the village being destroyed. As well as not knowing how many people were in the village, he knew that bringing in that level of fire power would not have helped our mission to gain intelligence in the region.

*

After breakfast the following morning, we sat in position and stayed put. The warlord to the north was talking to the Americans, and had told them that we'd run into one of his outposts and killed his men. He was readying a force to come out and kill us. The Americans told him not to. 'If you go anywhere past this line here,' they said, indicating a northern line on the map, 'we're going to bomb you.'

We ended up making our way down quite close to the Iranian border. The Iranians stood to. The speed at which we were moving made it seem like we were a large force, so the Iranians wouldn't have known we were just one unit. They would have had intelligence assets seeing who we were, but they were still ready in case anything happened.

After two or three days on the move, we harboured up overnight in a small basin surrounded by high hills. The basin had a narrow access point that opened out onto the plains below. It was there that we discovered we'd been followed the whole way.

Just as we were having breakfast, we saw two vehicles further down the mountain. They were stopping and starting and crossing over each other's paths. On our way to camp, we'd tried to be a little bit deceptive by breaking our tracks and going back and forth. The drivers of these two vehicles were clearly linking up where our tracks had gone, so we knew it was us they were looking for.

When they finally saw where we were camped, they sent one of the vehicles up to a little bit of dead ground that we couldn't see.

The Oracle went down with a couple of guys and his interpreter to talk to them.

'Was it you guys that we were firing at three days ago?' the interpreter asked.

'Maybe,' came the reply. 'Who are you?'

As if the Oracle was going to tell them! They might as well have asked, 'Do you want to die today?'

Then the Afghani guy said, 'My commander wants to have a meeting with you out there.' He gestured towards the southern side of the mountain range. 'Be there in 30 minutes.'

After agreeing, the Oracle came back and informed us of the meeting. We decided to split ourselves up, so we had one group in fire support and the other group – which I was a part of, on my bike – drove off and set up further down the mountain. Then, at the appointed time, two vehicles drove up in front of our position. In one was a guy who was clearly the commander. He was standing up on the back of this old Russian four-by-four and wore an old Russian army uniform complete with big epaulettes and shiny hat. He looked absolutely classic. He was clearly there on behalf of one of the warlords.

We had four vehicles – one facing to the rear and three at the front – and we had him outgunned. We also had our outriders – of which I was one – on the flanks watching him. Then I turned and saw some activity on the horizon, so I radioed: 'I can see a dust plume coming from the west.' Then there were two dust plumes, then three, then ten. I lost count at about 24. I got back on the radio: 'There's a huge amount of activity happening behind us.'

'Roger that.'

Suddenly, all these vehicles appeared, racing around the side of us. There must have been about 100 of these guys. They had all these technicals – utes with machine guns on top – and two flatbed trucks with anti-aircraft guns on them, so they had air defence sorted out.

Here we go, I thought. *It's on now.*

As all this was happening, the commander stayed standing on the back of his truck, keeping his cool. Then all of his men got off their vehicles, looking similarly relaxed.

Meanwhile, the Oracle was quietly giving instructions. We all had our targets sorted out, starting off with the heavy weapons. If it was going to kick off, it was pretty clear that it was going to be a massacre for both sides – and all I had for cover was my motorbike!

Then the Oracle went out into the open, alongside the interpreter, who must have been absolutely bricking it. That's when the commander finally got off his truck. He walked right up to the Oracle, close enough to start pushing him in the chest and shouting at him. The Oracle stood his ground, gently pushing the commander back and encouraging him to take it down a notch, so that they could speak more rationally. If he didn't, the Oracle calmly explained – and I'm paraphrasing – 'a big bird in the sky will come and shit on your head'. And, just as the Oracle said this, a Spectre AC-130 happened to fly over us.

The guys standing around the technicals had an instant reaction, with some of them backing off and even making for their vehicles.

The Spectre gunship didn't generally appear during the day, but it was on its way back from a mission and had come in because we were miles away from any other support.

Meanwhile, the Oracle had decided he wanted to bring our fire support in a bit closer. But, as one of our vehicles was moving in, it hit an old Russian landmine. The map we had of the area had showed there were landmines, but that they were out to the west – it turned out that map was 20 years old, and over time the mines had moved down the mountain as it eroded. The mine the vehicle hit was a small anti-personnel one, maybe one or two kilograms, and it hit the driver. His leg was badly injured. The guy in the turret flew out and hit the ground, smashing his head. The other guy also got thrown out of the vehicle.

I had the safety off on my weapon, and when I heard the boom, I turned to look. I started taking the tension up on the trigger at the same time as my brain was telling me that was probably the trigger for them to engage us. I thought the Afghani guys who'd had the meeting with the Oracle had laid the mine, and that it was a signal for them to start opening up on us. But, before I opened fire, I looked at these guys – and I saw that they were confused by what had happened. They obviously had no idea what was going on.

That landmine going off actually helped to defuse the situation. As a result of both that and the Spectre's low pass, the warlord's men all eventually piled back into their vehicles and left.

Our three guys who'd hit the landmine were in need of medical assistance, so I hopped back on the motorbike, grabbed the medic and said to him, 'Mate, I'm just going to ride you in there really fast. If we connect with something, hopefully the detonator will be delayed and worst-case scenario it'll blow the rear tyre off, but we'll be good.' We both laughed. It was a dumb rationale, and we knew it, but off we went, into the minefield, where I dropped him off before riding really fast back out again.

When I got back, we went through our mine drill, got everyone out as far as we could, then set up shop in the area. We were that far away that it took two hours for the helicopter to come in, but the medics managed to wrap up the driver's injured leg and keep him alive. He and the two gunners were all in shock, and the driver ended up getting medevaced to Germany, where his lower leg was amputated below the knee.

Once everyone was safely out of the area, we went in and laid some charges on the vehicle and blew it up and watched it burn.

*

We couldn't go far for a few days because we were running low on fuel. A call had been made for a resupply, but the assets required to make it happen were doing other things that had higher priority, so we had to wait. Until the resupp came, we balanced out our fuel tanks by making sure each vehicle had a quarter of a tank.

During this time, we came across a military outpost with just one person. When our interpreter asked who he was and what he was doing, he said he was a member of the ANA, but he could have been Taliban for all we knew. We gave him something to eat and asked if he had any information for us. He took us up and showed us the site of a massive cache of ammunitions just up the valley – it was buried, and it was big.

Then the other motorbike rider and I went to drop the ANA guy back at his outpost. On the way I noticed some things sticking out of the ground, but I didn't think too much about them. When we got back to the patrol, the Oracle was sitting there laughing. 'What's so funny?' I asked as I got off the bike.

'I've got some bad news,' he replied.

'What's that?'

'We're in the middle of another minefield.'

'What?' Then I thought for a moment. 'I did see some metal things on the ground ...'

'Yeah, they were probably mines. We're going to have a very slow trip out again tomorrow.'

*

The following day, swinging metal detectors the whole way, we managed to get the entire convoy safely out of the minefield. Then we took care of the large ammunitions cache, and pulled as much as we could out of it.

After that, the resupp finally arrived – as well as fuel, they brought water (which we were also running low on), food and four explosive ordnance disposal guys (two Kiwis and two

Americans) with additional explosives to destroy the cache. We had no idea who the arms belonged to – they might have been Taliban, or they could have been the warlords' – but we took out a considerable amount of firepower, much of which was still in pretty good nick.

Then we headed all the way south to Farah, which is close to the Iranian border. While there, we met with the governor, as we were the first Western forces to have gone there. At that time, some areas were still autonomous and pretty functional. They had their own government and security forces, and no Taliban presence. Farah was one of them, and the governor was more than happy to let us use his airfield for an extraction. By the time we finally returned to base, we'd been out for three and a half weeks. We were all skinny, with massively long beards.

About a week earlier, we'd noticed the locals gathering firewood and now we suddenly learnt why. As though a switch had been flicked, the temperature dropped dramatically and winter arrived with a punch. The heat was no longer an issue, because the rain and snow had taken its place.

*

On long-range patrols, we sometimes came across Bedouins. They had massive tents, a huge number of goats and quite ferocious guard dogs. They'd shift campsites in the middle of the night because it was a lot cooler then, so we'd often pick up their movements through our NVGs.

During the summer they'd go up to their high camps in the mountains, and in the winter they'd be in their low camps nearer the cities. No one messed with them, because they didn't get involved in politics. They were just out in the middle of nowhere doing their thing.

On one patrol when we were a long way from anywhere, we laid up above a Bedouin camp. Unusually, the camp consisted of just one tent and a couple of goats. We hadn't been in position long before two boys came up to us. One would have been 14 and the other maybe 11. They were emaciated and filthy, and told the interpreter that they hadn't had food in a while. In a lot of those rural areas deep inside the country, it could be really hard to get food. There was nothing to hunt and the land won't grow anything much.

We loaded the two boys up with ration packs and some onions and potatoes from our supplies, hoping it might give them a bit of respite from the hunger. It wasn't enough, but it was all we could really do.

*

The last job we did before heading home to New Zealand was a bit of a change of scene from long patrols. The then-Minister of Foreign Affairs, Phil Goff, was visiting Afghanistan for a couple of days in early December, and our squadron was tasked with providing his security detail while he was in Kabul.

Being in Kabul was hugely different from what we'd experienced when we were based out of Kandahar. Where Kandahar was basically a suburb at the time, Kabul was a big, bustling, proper city. But there were always curfews, so the streets were clear at nights.

While there, we stayed at the Intercontinental Hotel. It was the country's first luxury hotel, and opened in 1969, back when Afghanistan still had a king. Since then, it's provided accommodation for international visitors, and a base for whoever is running the country at the time. As part of our role, we memorised the layout of the hotel. It sits on a hill in Kārte Parwān, to the west of the city centre, and is semi busy with 200 rooms, a swimming pool, and a grand dining room. Aircrew as well as local and foreign dignitaries stayed there. It wasn't too bad, but it was dated; adequate, but I wouldn't call it flash.

During his visit, the Minister for Foreign Affairs met with several groups: President Karzai, the Afghan foreign minister, the International Security Assistance Force (ISAF) commander, people from the UN and Kiwi troops on the ground. While he was with the representative of the UN secretary-general, we got to meet some of the other UN staff ourselves. One of the senior staff was a Kiwi, so a couple of us took the opportunity to tell her about some of the things we'd experienced while out on patrol. We told her the story about the malnourished Bedouin boys we'd given food to, then asked her how far the UN went out with their aid.

'As far as we can with the vehicles,' she replied. 'But that's only so far, because we don't go in armed and there's so many bandits on the roads.'

'What about flying in?'

'We don't have aircraft.'

All that money, I thought. *They could have bought some helicopters.*

It was all well and good giving aid to the people who were close, but we knew the people who really needed it were further out. We'd been out there and seen it for ourselves. Looking after people needs to be at the forefront, especially when the fighting is about ideology. The most important thing for any of us – UN or SAS – should be to make sure the people who need help get it.

6

BREAD AND WATER

IT WAS AFTER COMING back from Afghanistan that I started to realise there was a huge difference between my experiences and the experiences of some of the other people in my life. Whenever I tried to talk about what I was up to with my family or friends from outside the squadron, I noticed they'd listen for a while ... then change the subject. It felt like they didn't really care about where I'd been or what I'd been doing.

So I stopped talking about it with them. Someone would say, 'So what have you been up to?' and I'd just reply, 'Oh, you know, this and that ...' and then the conversation would just move on to other things. I'd sit there silently, unable to connect with what they were talking about. The things that mattered in their lives were so far away from what was going on in my life. It felt like we were on different planets, and I gradually fell out of the loop with them.

It was easier to just hang around with the people who did know and understand what my life was like: the boys in the squadron. They'd either been there with me, or they'd been through it themselves. I could look them in the eye knowing that they'd understand. There was already a high level of trust between us, so this seemed like a natural progression.

The regiment had a strong culture, and you always knew where you stood. As well as trust, expectation was a big thing. The expectation that you'd perform well, and that you'd expect others to do the same. Spending most of my time with the boys in the regiment meant that this level of expectation, the constant drive to always go harder, bled into my personal life. When I wasn't at work, I would 'relax' by doing stuff like going skydiving all weekend. On my way down to the airfield at Mercer, I'd be psyching myself up. 'I wonder if I can do ten jumps?' I'd ask myself. 'Yeah! I'm going to see if I can!'

I was just continually looking for the next challenge, the next rush. And, in the environment I was in, it wasn't difficult. I could always find something to put my sympathetic nervous system into that fight-or-flight mode. I was a young fella, with tonnes of energy, and the squadron provided me with the sort of mates who wanted the same kinds of adventures as I did. The hard stuff was the humility, but the humour was definitely there, too – there was always a lot of laughing and joking around.

Around the time I got back from Afghanistan, a guy called Steve Askin joined the squadron. Straight away, he started sticking out because he was really confident, fit and competitive – even in the context of a group of extremely fit and competitive people, he was at the high end of the scale. He was always up for a challenge – and a bit of humour. Once he started to settle in to squadron life, I saw that he was quite a mischievous guy too.

One night, he and another guy, Eel, were in the bar at the camp and decided they were hungry. But when they went around and tried to get into the kitchen, they found it was locked. They were from mountain troop, so they got up on the roof, found a skylight, opened it and rappelled in. Then, once they were in the kitchen, they cooked a feed, didn't clean up, then left again.

When the CO got wind of it, Steve and Eel fronted up straight away. The CO did not see the humorous side of their shenanigans. He was really pissed off. There had to be consequences, and there were: Steve and Eel had their belts and berets removed, then they were escorted down to military prison in Christchurch, where they were told that they had to do their time well or they wouldn't be coming back.

A military prison is not like a normal prison. They shave your hair down to a number two, as though you are on basic training, and the daily physical training is brutal. They also muck you around the whole time you're there. For example, you might get a nugget tin that's spraypainted black and have to scrub all the paint off with a scourer in time to present it to the orderly on duty before lights-out. The orderly would then grab the tins so they could all be repainted so you could repeat the process.

Steve and Eel behaved themselves down there, and when they did eventually return a month later, we welcomed them back with a re-enactment. We set up some ropes on a truck, put some food down below, then made Steve and Eel run through the whole performance again – this time in front of all the boys. Don't get me wrong. We didn't advocate what they'd done … but the culture was to take the piss, and we certainly did that!

*

On one training exercise in early 2004, we had a new guy join the Parachute Training Support Unit. He was a parachute instructor from Brize Norton, the RAF's parachute training school, and when I asked if he'd done tandem before, he said he had. I took him at his word, but gave him the full brief before we jumped anyway: 'I'm just going to reiterate that you need to hang in the harness once we are at the ramp and let me take control of the exit so we fly stable out of the aircraft.'

The ramp on a Herc is right at the back, and if you're standing by the door getting ready to jump with a person on your front, you want them to hang in the harness so you can take their weight. This allows you to control the exit. If the person in front straightens their legs, they'll end up taking control of the exit just as your feet leave the ramp – and the consequences of that could be fatal, particularly at night with full equipment.

He nodded, and a patrol went ahead of us, then we moved up to the ramp. It was the middle of the night, so it was pitch black outside, and everything happened really quickly – you can't muck around up there. We had maybe 15 seconds to get everyone out. We were loaded up with a pack front and rear, rifles, NVGs and helmet – and as soon as this guy and I got to the edge of the ramp, I shouted, 'Ready, set, go!'

But the second my feet left the ramp I could feel that he'd taken control of the exit. He'd pushed off the aircraft. We went over and instantly came off centre, then started going into a flat side spin.

I'd trained for unstable exits like this, but I wasn't thrilled to be dealing with it. Especially not in the dark. After having a bit of a moment, I thought, *OK, I've just got to sort myself out. How are we orientated?*

On one side, I had a drogue chute, which I needed to throw once we were stable in order to keep us stable. It's also designed to slow you down and keep you at a manageable terminal velocity (just under 200 kilometres an hour) and to deploy the main parachute when that's released with a pull cord. I knew we'd get up to a high freefall speed of around 322 kilometres per hour really fast, and then when I pulled the parachute there was the possibility of a violent opening. This would cause significant dynamic pressure on the canopy and harness, which could cause the suspension lines or canopy to tear – and possible physical injury to us due to the sudden decrease in speed.

We were spinning drogue side up, so I threw the drogue and that righted us, but we were still spinning. I managed to slow the spin by pushing my arm down on the air in the opposite direction of the spin, and then I could see the patrol below us, illuminated with Cyalume sticks, so I checked our height – we were just about at opening height, so I pulled the parachute open. We landed safely on Ohakea airfield – but things could have so easily gone the other way. If I'd been on the other side when we came out, I would have had to try to throw the drogue around the packs, and hope that it didn't wrap around them. If the drogue chute had wrapped around the packs, I would have had to release the reserve parachute and hoped it cleared. That was a big lesson for me. It reminded me, in that particular context, that the reaper was always out there and if you opened the door, he would step right in.

A couple of times during night jumps, things went from bad to worse for me, but rectifying the issues through process gave me faith in both my own abilities and in the drills that we had been taught. I also recognised I was fairly calm in these type of tricky situations – something I later came to understand as being in flow, right there in the present moment, focusing on nothing else.

*

We'd come back from Afghanistan in late 2002, and the following March US-led coalition forces had invaded Iraq. One consequence of this was a reduction in the number of coalition boots on the ground in Afghanistan – something the Taliban and Al-Qaeda took advantage of by beginning to rebuild their forces. So, with the Afghan presidential elections due to take place in October 2004, the US government requested their New Zealand counterparts deploy the SAS to assist with reconnaissance work and making sure the polling booths remained open and protected.

We got word that we were likely to be deployed, but we couldn't tell anyone because we didn't know for sure. Then, one Thursday in February 2004, we went into a meeting and were informed that we'd be leaving the following Monday. The CO knew the operation was coming up but could not tell us until the green light was given by government. That weekend, I caught up with my family, then gave Mum a call the night before I left. And then we were on our way.

The troop commander on that deployment was a guy called Craig Wilson, who I knew well, and who later went on to author the book *Bravo Kiwi*. I'd been promoted to corporal, and was the Outrider Lead, while Steve was the second outrider. Also with us were Ricardo and Rob, plus Willie Apiata.

It was my first time working with Steve, and he was pretty good – even if we did knock heads a bit! That's to be expected in the regiment, though. The way I saw it, he was teaching me a lesson because I'd always been as strong-minded as he was. It was a taste of my own medicine. We ended up working well together, and were pretty much joined at the hip through that tour.

Once again, we were based at our camp in Kandahar, but this time we were accommodated in a secure area along with US special forces units. By this time, there was a functioning mess and we had a supply of fresh food coming in. It was a welcome upgrade from our last deployment, even if it was still pretty rough. A bit more money was coming in by this stage, because the government had started to see our worth. They were hearing from other countries' special forces that we were doing some good stuff, and it was paying off.

Even our motorbikes had been upgraded. This time we were on KTM 525s, which were more powerful than the Kawasakis and specifically built for enduro riding. They ate up the hills and mountains with ease, and maintained power at altitude – we rode around in the mountains at heights of 4,000 metres above sea level, in the snow, with no problems at all. We could do whatever we wanted on those 525s, and it was no effort. Those bikes were worth their weight in gold.

*

Just as we had on our first deployment, we arrived and got into things slowly. After doing some training, we headed out further afield. Our goal on this deployment was to engage with local leaders in order to find out where the Taliban were.

We went out for two or three weeks at a time, then came back for a week, before heading out again. And we just kept doing that for six months. We'd soon grown massive beards and long hair, so we fitted in pretty well with the locals! Some of the areas we went into were pretty hostile, and it wasn't uncommon for people to take potshots at us every now and again. Steve and I would be riding along, and we'd have the odd round flying at us.

In early June, we headed out on a long-range patrol with the goal of getting into a big valley that American special forces had been trying to access with little success. They wanted to meet with the locals, and had been going in from the south in their technicals but never made it very far because they'd get hit every time, just a couple of kilometres in. They started losing guys, but they weren't set up for long-range missions so they just kept doing the same thing.

We looked at that pattern, and were like, 'Well, forget that.' Instead, we opted to take three or four days going up and around the mountain range, so we could come in from the northern end. The local militia would never know we were coming, because they'd got so used to the Americans coming in from the south.

It was the middle of summer, with daytime temperatures over 40 degrees Celsius, so we travelled at night, both for safety and to avoid the heat. Our route took us through both Hazara and Pashtun territory. The former was easy for us, as we got on well with the Hazara, but the Pashtun territory was another story; we had to go through some very unfriendly villages there. In one, the main marketplace was only a couple of metres wide, and on either side were raised mud platforms with market stalls on top. This meant you could either drive down the centre of the market (a tight fit in the Humvees), or walk along the footpaths on either side. I was driving one of the Humvees as a vehicle commander, and as I drove through the market a guy ran out of one of the shops towards us. I didn't see him, but one of our gunners did. He could see something in the guy's hand – he thought it might have been a knife, but he wasn't 100 per cent sure. Then, before the gunner responded, two more local guys appeared and grabbed the would-be attacker, pulling him back into the shop.

The gunner looked at me. 'Mate, I'm pretty sure that guy had a knife. And he was going to stab you in the head with it.'

I hadn't even seen the guy. 'Where did he go?' I asked, and the gunner pointed to the shop.

I radioed for the convoy to stop so I could investigate, then got out of the Humvee and went into the shop with our interpreter. Inside, a bunch of men were sitting down. They all looked straight at me.

'What are you guys doing?' the interpreter asked for me.

One was visibly irritated, but the others talked to our interpreter. Once they'd finished explaining, the interpreter turned back to me. 'They say that guy there is upset because his brother was killed by coalition forces. He wanted to get his revenge.'

It was my head he'd been aiming the knife at, but even I could understand why this guy had responded the way he had, given what had happened to him. I asked the interpreter to explain to the men gathered that, without knowing the circumstances around the man's brother's death we, in particular, would not engage unless threatened. Then we moved on.

*

We carried on around the mountain range, and as soon as we moved into the valley from its northern end the local militia started shooting up in the air to let everyone know that we were coming. But, since they were used to the American forces trying to gain access from the south, they hadn't put bombs, mines or improvised explosive devices (IEDs) in the road. So we drove all the way in, straight to the village where we wanted to make contact with the local leader.

Once we arrived, we moved very slowly into the village itself. Everyone seemed to be looking at us, giving us the evils. We didn't find the leader, so we told the locals through our interpreters that we were going to station ourselves up on a hill about a kilometre out of town. 'We'll be there for the next couple of days,' we said. 'If anyone's got any information for us, you can come up and tell us any time.'

Our interpreters were worth their weight in gold. They were either Afghan-Americans or Afghan locals, and had usually been with US special forces before they joined us. They were putting everything on the line, because if the Taliban found out they were working for us, there was a real chance they'd get their heads cut off.

The hill had two plateaus and provided us with a strong defensive position from which we could see what was happening in the village. We had three vehicles parked up on the top plateau, while the rest of us stayed down on the lower one. And, before the day was out, one guy did come up from the village. He pretended to give us information, but we knew that he was really only there to see how we were laid out.

When night fell, it was particularly dark as there was no moon, and this meant our NVGs weren't as useful as they'd normally be. It had been a really long day, so we were all tired. We sorted out sentry duty, and when it was my turn to get some rest I had no trouble falling asleep.

I was woken again in the wee hours – it must have been about 3am – by the sound of gunfire. I looked up, and there was a blanket of tracer coming over the top of the hill. If anyone had poked their head over that hill, it would have been taken off.

Whenever we slept on patrol, we used our webbing as a pillow, so that we could just put it on and go when we woke up. We also slept in our uniforms, with our boots on, so that we could start fighting straight away if anything happened. But I was still in my sleeping bag as I tried to figure out what was going on. *Is that us firing*, I wondered, *or are we getting contacted from over there?*

I peered down the hill, trying to see muzzle flashes out in the opposite direction, but there was nothing. I switched my radio on, and the comms started. We could see all these rocket-propelled grenades (RPGs) getting fired off the other side of the hill. It was quite high, but some were accurate and slammed into a couple of our vehicles.

We were all on our feet by now. Since it was such a heavy contact, the troop commander told everyone to get up on the hill and start helping out. We had an American special tactics guy with us who was a gunner, but he was on the radio, calling in their close air support. Since he wasn't operating a weapons system, I got on it instead.

The initial fire had been concentrated on one of the vehicles up on the top plateau. In it was Willie, Rob and Tom, and they'd been hit by RPGs and heavy machine-gun fire. Rob had been shot through the arm, and his brachial artery – the major blood vessel in the upper arm – was hit. He was at risk of bleeding out and dying. They were under fire and their vehicle was up in flames, but Willie and the other guy still managed to apply a tourniquet to Rob's wound. Then they had to get him out to one of the other vehicles, so he could be treated by the patrol medic, but they were still under heavy fire. Rob tried to run for safety, but he'd lost so much blood that he just collapsed. So Willie scooped him up, put him over his shoulders, and ran for safety. All three men ended up surviving (and Willie was later awarded the Victoria Cross for his actions).

Meanwhile, we were still engaging with the people who'd done their best to kill our three counterparts. They'd started moving up the hill, and had a fire-support team over the other side of the mountain that had opened up on us with automatic weapons, pinning us down.

My mate Ricardo came over with his vehicle at exactly the right time. He and his top gunner started engaging as they were manoeuvring up the side of the hill, and killed the commander and one of the other soldiers.

Taking out the commander turned out to be a decisive move. Once he was gone, the rest of the fighters started withdrawing, because they had no one to direct them. It was as simple as that.

But they'd put a whole lot of fallback positions in place – they'd hidden little caches of weapons and ammunition all the way down the valley that they used to engage us as they withdrew.

I got up on the weapons system, which was a Mk 19 automatic grenade launcher. At that time, we didn't have any real night-vision weapon-sight capability. The best we had was a first-generation PEQ-2 laser sight that we'd screwed onto the barrel ad hoc because we didn't have any mounting systems. Ricardo was on them, so he started firing, but he had an old Kite sight that wasn't great at range, and he couldn't see much. He could just see them withdrawing and firing and manoeuvring back, so he said, 'Just follow my tracer, man.' I nodded, and put the lasers on them, then started firing a volley of 40-millimetre grenades in their direction.

They were still moving, and eventually they disappeared round a corner.

Then all of a sudden I saw this Toyota Corolla on the other side of the bank and realised the fire-support group was trying to escape. Weirdly, they had their headlights on. They were also deliberately driving about from left to right. *How am I going to do this?* I thought. Trying to hit a moving target is difficult, and despite my best efforts they eventually disappeared off behind the mountain in that Corolla.

By this time, the sun was starting to rise, so the troop divided up. One half stayed on site to secure the position, while the other half headed out to try to capture some of the combatants. I went out with them to see if I could find the Corolla, and just as we got down to the road we spotted it driving along. Then the driver saw us too, came to a halt, and all these guys hopped out and ran into the village, then the car drove off again.

We had a B1 bomber on station by then, and the special tactics guys asked our troop commander if he wanted them to take the car out. 'Yes,' he replied. 'Take it out. They're hostiles.' But then the special tactics guys asked for the grid reference – they only had bombs and not guided missiles – and we didn't have it. There was no point in our air cover just lobbing a bomb out and hoping it hit the right place. So our commander ultimately decided that we'd have to forget about the vehicle.

*

We went off to clear out the village, putting in a security cordon then going from house to house looking for anyone who had been involved in the attack. It was a slow process. We'd been at it for about an hour when Seamus Potak, our group commander, said, 'We'll just stop here, lads, and take a quick drink.'

While we were all standing there, this lady walked up to us carrying a cow's stomach full of water and offered it to us. Seamus was right into down and dirty stuff like that. 'Yeah, I'd love some of that water!' he said, and took a swig out of the stomach, then offered it to the rest of us. 'No thanks, mate,' I replied when he held it up to me. 'I don't want to get giardia!'

Then some more of the local women came over, and they had bread, which the rest of us were more keen on than the cow's stomach. So we sat there for a moment, just eating bread and chilling out with these local women.

Nine times out of ten, the people in these villages – and the women especially – didn't want to know about what the Taliban was up to. They were not interested in the fighting. They just wanted to be left in peace to get on with their lives. Sure, there were some who were hardcore into it, but that was often because they'd had family members killed and that led them to join the cause. But generally, people didn't want anything to do with it. They'd rather share their bread and water in peace.

*

It took us half a day to clear the village. We'd go into each house and tell everyone to get down while we cleared the compound. Often, the women would just stand there and watch us. They didn't get down on the ground, but that wasn't surprising, as they didn't understand English and our interpreters didn't follow along while we were clearing. And we weren't shouting or aggressive, so the women didn't find us particularly threatening.

We'd do a quick search and clearance of each compound, and if we didn't find anything we just kept going. This was another difference between Kiwis and other nations. We were a special forces unit – a surgical tool. If someone was going to be a threat, they'd show themselves as a threat and that's when we'd deal with it. Otherwise, we would move on.

In one compound, I heard a dog barking and a woman yelling, so I gave the nod to the guy I was with to open the door, and we went in. I went left while he went right, and immediately this dog – which had been bred to kill wolves and stood at hip height – ran straight for me. Realising I was in trouble, I started shooting at it before it got the chance to take my legs out. I shot it in the head, but it had so much momentum that it kept running, then stumbled and hit my feet. Dogs were a real problem over there, particularly if they had rabies. They could easily rip you to bits.

*

We finally finished clearing the village, but we hadn't ended up getting much in the way of intel besides finding out where our attackers had done their planning, because they'd left their map model in one of the buildings.

Back up at the position where the ambush had occurred, we collected the weapons and ammunition that had been left behind, then made them safe and put them in our vehicles. Next, Steve and I did DNA swabs on the bodies of the assault-group commander and the fighter who had been killed. These samples were used to positively identify the men by connecting them back to their family, so it could be proved that they'd been taken off the battlefield.

Finally, we took the bodies back to the village. We dropped them off, talked to the villagers and got them to verify who the men were. They weren't too happy about it, understandably. However, at the end of the day, these guys had tried to kill us. They took that risk. And we didn't have to bring them back to the villagers, but that was another difference between New Zealanders and everyone else.

*

We eventually moved on to another village in the same region, and as we left it early one afternoon we decided to split call signs. My call sign was going to head south, to have a bit of a look further down the valley, while the other call sign would stay in place and support us if we needed it. But we'd only just started making our way down the valley when we got a call on the radio: 'Hold your position.' So we went into all-round defence, and had a bit of lunch while we waited for more info.

It turned out that a coalition intelligence officer had got word from his local source that an ambush had been set up just down the road, and was there to take out coalition forces in the area. The intelligence officer had rung our headquarters in Kandahar with this intel, and our headquarters had then radioed us to tell us to stop. That message had literally saved our lives. The road we'd been about to drive down had been lined with 105-millimetre artillery shells – one could take out a vehicle no worries, and they had four of them on that road.

Once we learnt all this, we just sat there for a bit, playing coy so as not to give the game away. People were driving past us on bikes, pretending they were going about their daily life, but really they were just checking us out.

Late in the afternoon, we returned to the village and rendezvoused with the other call sign, then we picked a spot to spend the night. It was up a hill, but it had a bit of a bowl, so we could get into a really good defensive position. It was quite open and there was a little entrance to it. There was a mountain range in front of us, and to our right were the Pashtun areas – the badlands – while to our left was where the Hazaras were. Between them was a line of rocks indicating the border between them, and if anyone crossed it, that was it for them. We were on the Pashtun side of that line.

That night, we got word from the Americans that the Pashtun were going to attack us, so we started getting in position. While that was happening, we also cooked dinner, pretending everything was business as usual. Meanwhile, the locals put up a command-and-control element on the hill, and sat there watching us. Soon, buses and trucks started arriving, and all these guys who came off them were walking along with weapons.

It looked like it was going to be a big night ...

When they started moving into position, we decided it was time to get some jets on station to provide cover for us. The Afghan fighters had surrounded us, and some would have only been about 150 metres away. They were lower down the hill, so we had them all covered and knew exactly where they were – but, for some reason, we were getting word not to engage with them. We could get amongst it if they attacked us, we were told, but otherwise we were not to do anything. Something was obviously going on at another level that we weren't privy to.

It was really hard to just sit there and do nothing. The jets were at 20,000 feet, and were putting infrared spotlights on people they could see moving down in front of us. I was on a forward sentry, just waiting and watching all night.

Eventually, dawn broke, and we were told to leave the area, so we drove out without being contacted. It was a very strange scenario.

For the next two days – until we were out of their territory – we were followed by a couple of motorbikes that were just keeping tabs on us. And we kept tabs on their chatter. They were thinking about how to put ambushes in front of us, but we just kept the speed on so they couldn't do anything. There was a lot of that sort of game-playing that went on, but ultimately we all got out and got back to Kandahar safely.

7

A CHANGE OF SCENE

BACK IN NEW ZEALAND after six months away, it took a bit for me to ease back into the real world. This time, I was living in my own house rather than at the camp, and it was a real adjustment. One thing that struck me was that, when we were out on operations – especially on mobility in the badlands – we always had a sentry on, which meant I always had someone watching my back. Once I got home, I didn't have that. As a result, I was constantly watching my own back. If I went into a café, I'd sit with my back against the wall so I could scan for threats and react. Even when I was walking down the street, I would be hyperaware of anything that was happening around me, just in case I needed to go from zero to hero in a heartbeat. It was the sort of thing that had been drummed into me through repetitive training, and I found I couldn't just turn it off.

Another presidential election was due to be held in Afghanistan in 2005, and the regiment was once again deployed to do long-range reconnaissance work, but this time I didn't go. And the squadron that did go ended up being the last off-shore deployment until 2009.

I spent the next few years based at Papakura, but I was away a lot, doing training and exercises all over the country. Then, when I was back home, I would spend my time trying to rest and catch up on the things I wanted to do. I was close to my family, but I only saw them a handful of times during those years. I talked to Mum on the phone more often, but that distance was still there between me and the rest of the family. I noticed they were having family dinners and get-togethers without me, and that hurt a little bit. I know now it was because I wasn't forthcoming with my movements – I didn't tell them when I was going away, so they didn't always know whether I was around or not.

No one really knew how to navigate the distance between us. I felt like my work, and especially the things I'd done in Afghanistan, had given me this higher strategic purpose. I'd done some pretty significant things with some pretty significant people, but that wasn't something many people could understand. And whenever I tried to talk about it, I felt like it got brushed off. I took it pretty hard. So I stuck with my approach of replying 'not much' whenever someone asked me what I'd been up to. Of course that wasn't true – I had heaps going on – but I just didn't ever feel like I could be open and honest about it, because no one outside of the regiment was interested or would understand.

Sometimes I wondered whether what I was experiencing might have been more interesting if I was a high-performance sportsperson instead of in the SAS. There are some ways that being in the regiment is like being on a top sports team – they're both incredibly demanding environments that drive participants to perform at their absolute upper limits. You're expected to operate at a different level. That's what your training is all about, and it's what you do at work all day. But no professional sportsperson in the world has ever had to make it through a selection process like the one for the special forces – and sportspeople can also rely on getting the right nutrition and enough sleep! That's the main difference between elite athletes and special forces soldiers, I guess: the regiment needs people who can perform at the top of their game, in the worst conditions. The bar is set extremely high. That's why such a small portion of the global population will ever become special forces soldiers.

Of course those of us in the regiment knew what we'd been through to get there, and what we had to do to stay there. But it could sometimes feel like we were the *only* ones who knew it. The only ones who appreciated just how hard it was, and what an achievement it was. When we were sent on operations, it was usually to places far from home. Places like Afghanistan, or countries in the Middle East, which face very different problems from what New Zealand was up against. Our country is so fortunate in the sense that no one's really looking at us. When it comes to wars and conflict, it often feels like we're last on the list: 'Ah, we'll get to you guys later!'

But this is where some of the distance comes from between special forces soldiers and the general public. Lots of guys come back from operations and discover, just like I did, that their families are so far removed from what they've seen and been through that they'll never understand what it was like. When the general public hears that our special forces are over in war-torn places, they can be like, 'Yeah, whatever ...' and don't give it any more thought than that. They don't really understand that, although we might be a small group, we're vital. There's a real misconception that SAS soldiers are solely designed to kill people. The reality is we are designed to save people. We're essentially saving people from the world's bullies. Bullies who have no problems killing innocent civilians who cannot defend themselves. That is when we step in to put them in check and make sure they cannot force their influence and ideology on people who do not care for it. We don't train thousands of hours, day and night for any other reason.

Not being able to talk about what you're living through with the people you are closest to can have a really negative impact on your mental health. That's why the boys lean on the boys. It's also why networks like No Duff have been created. Taking its name from the military term meaning 'this is not a drill', No Duff is basically a network of members and ex-members of the armed forces who can reach out to each other on social media and other means. If one of us sees or hears that another member is struggling or worse, we can put a call out to see if there's anyone nearby who can help and support. And this could be anywhere in the world. It's all entirely voluntary. The aim is simply to make sure that if a soldier, sailor or airman has landed on hard times, there is a support network there that will wrap around that person.

*

Whatever environment we went into, we had to have a combination of people with different specialist skills. We'd have an advanced medic, an advanced communicator, a tracker, an advanced demolitions guy – all the environmental skills were there, so that we could be self-sustaining and do whatever we needed to, anywhere we were sent. It was really dynamic. Each patrol was comprised of people from all the different troops, so they'd all have a broad range of skills. And, on training exercises, we'd put all those skills together. Whatever we were doing, we were led by the relevant experts.

So, we might do an exercise that looked like this: parachute out of the back of a Herc and land in the sea, then get onto a boat and travel towards a target, or get dropped off some distance from the coast and have to swim with fins to land, then climb some cliffs. With all your gear. In the middle of the night.

I was a qualified jumpmaster, so on an exercise like this I would check everyone off before they jumped out of the aircraft. It was on me until everyone was out of the plane. Then, once we hit the water, the leadership changed hands to the water specialist, who'd be in charge until we made landfall. Then, if we landed on an island with sheer cliffs, someone from a mountain troop would take over as leader while we all climbed up to the top.

Once we were all in place, we'd go on patrol, and we were all proficient at that. The patrol might have a tracker, and there'd also be an advanced demolition guy, but everyone knew how to do demolitions so they could construct the charges and blow them.

Once that had been done, we'd get out – maybe by boat, maybe by helicopter, maybe up over a mountain. Whatever the setting, we all had to have the skills to traverse it.

And that's why, between deployments, we were constantly training. The scope of flexibility was huge, and keeping on top of these high-level skills was a massive job. It was vital that we were all able to assimilate information quickly, so we could get up to speed without delay. That way, if an operation came up, we were able to pick up our gear and jump in and do it well even at the shortest notice.

*

I spent a few months in 2006 freefall training with the US special forces. The first part of this was a four-week-long military freefall course, which included a week in a vertical wind tunnel called the Matis in North Carolina. It was an older type of wind tunnel, one of the first wind tunnels built, and it had these massive propellers spinning below you that blew air through a catch mat and allowed you to fly. Wind-tunnel training enabled us to practise flying without falling out of the sky.

From there, we headed to the US Army Yuma Proving Ground (YPG) in Arizona. YPG provides a series of specific environments for testing military equipment to make sure it performs no matter where it's deployed, and the Yuma Test Center (YTC) is one of the largest military installations in the world. The region boasts almost perfect testing and training conditions: clean air, low humidity, minimal rainfall (only about 80 millimetres a year) and sunny days (on average 350 a year).

Just seeing the assets that the US Army had here, and what was happening on base, was a real eye-opener. As I walked down the tarmac one day, I saw two F-22 stealth bombers. They'd only just gone into service a few months earlier, and I'd never seen anything like them. They didn't look real. They looked like some kind of mock-up of an aircraft.

The conditions were always good for jumping there, so we got in three solid weeks of jumping. Back in New Zealand, I'd spent so much time sitting in the ready room, waiting for the weather to be right. *It might happen ... Nope, not today. Come back tomorrow.* Here though, we were able to jump every day. We were in a CASA C-212, which is a smaller aircraft with a rear ramp. It couldn't mimic the speed of the Herc, but it could do everything else – and for much less money. We could do all the drills we needed to in it.

When I got over there, I'd already done my freefall course in New Zealand and had around 300 jumps under my belt, but I basically had to forget everything I'd been taught and just swing into the flow of it. The way they did things was similar, but different. They really had their shit squared away.

To pass the course, you had to be able to pack the specialised freefall parachute and know the procedures for jumping with all your combat gear, including weapons and NVGs. When it came to jumping, you had to be able to exit the aircraft in a variety of positions, and prove that you knew all the necessary emergency procedures – some of which I had recent experience of using! All of this was so that you could then do HALO and HAHO jumps from between 12,000 feet and 25,000 feet.

The tests all had practical applications. The first test was to jump out of the back of the plane and remain stable as you flew into a freefall position. Some guys just couldn't crack that one, so we lost about five people at that point. Next, you had to fly within a patrol formation at night, then make sure you tracked off into a clean space away from the rest of the patrol before pulling your parachute.

There was always an instructor at the front, leading the way, and one at the top, watching. You only had so many chances to pass: a pre-test, a test and a retest. A lot of guys pushed it right to the retest before passing. I found it interesting seeing how other forces measured up peer to peer. As for me, it was all about doing the work and getting it squared away as soon as possible. I made sure I always cracked it in the pretest. Another Kiwi guy had done the course before me, and he'd passed. So, in my mind, he'd set the expectation that, as a New Zealander, I would perform at the same level, if not better. I was also conscious of being a good representative – I wanted to make sure the other special forces people I was there with came away talking about New Zealand soldiers in a positive way.

*

Once I completed the freefall course, it was on to the military freefall jumpmaster's course. This was really just an extension of the earlier course, and I spent three weeks qualifying to check and dispatch personnel conducting HAHO and HALO parachute operations.

There was a lot more classroom work on this course, but I did manage to get a jump in on Anzac Day. Apart from being in the forces myself, Anzac Day has always had a special significance for me, as my great uncle – my mum's uncle – was killed serving in the New Zealand Army in Egypt during the Second World War. Man, that jump was gold. I was first out the door at the crack of dawn, and it doesn't get any better than that.

I returned to New Zealand with a better understanding of current military-freefall best practice, equipment used and a sharper skillset.

*

By May 2008, I'd been promoted to sergeant and I was assigned to my first overseas deployment since Afghanistan. This time, I was heading to the Middle East as a Personal Protection Officer (PPO) to New Zealand's Chief of Defence Force, Lieutenant General (now Sir) Jerry Mateparae.

The SAS is always called on to provide protection to politicians or government dignitaries making these sorts of high-threat or high-risk visits into war zones, and these PPO trips were always really full on. They were fast, complex and involved lots of logistical detail. I never slept much. But they were a great chance to get out and about, especially when there wasn't much going on.

Since PPOs need to be able to hold a conversation, be diplomatic and look professional, those of us selected for the role were also taught about etiquette – including which knives and forks to use. We even had a fashion advisor come in to tell us how to dress and when. This was all because you didn't ever want to outshine the VIP, but you also didn't want to *under*shine them. The goal was to find a happy medium, and we had to be able to adjust to that level as quickly as possible.

On this trip, Lieutenant General Mateparae was going to visit our troops in the Sinai Peninsula, Egypt and the United Arab Emirates over the course of a couple of weeks. I flew into Cairo ahead of him, and there I met with the Warrant Officer of Defence Force (WODF) and the defence attaché for Riyadh to discuss the plan for the whole trip. Then Lieutenant General Mateparae arrived, and we got on with business. He was great to work with, as he'd been in the regiment earlier in his career, so the mutual respect was there from the get-go.

One thing I learnt on that trip was just how hard the Chief of Defence Force works. We were sleeping bugger all, and Lieutenant General Mateparae would just get up and nail every meeting, every speech, every dinner, everything. I guess he'd done it so many times by then that he could just talk off the cuff. It was really impressive.

Once he'd gone to bed each night, I'd stay up for another hour planning for the next day. After two weeks of that, I was a wreck, even with all my SAS training! Lack of sleep aside, it was a really good trip – and definitely another side of the coin from the work I'd been doing in places like Afghanistan.

*

While we were in Cairo, we met with New Zealand embassy staff and I took the opportunity to ask them about how to get to the cemetery where my great-uncle was buried. 'You want to visit? We'll sort it all out for you,' they said – and they did, including a vehicle and an interpreter. I'll be forever grateful to them for doing that.

The Commonwealth War Cemetery at El Alamein is around 300 kilometres to the west of Cairo, and is the final resting place of 7,240 Commonwealth servicemen. Many of them – including my great-uncle, Private Ashton Herrick – died in the Battle of El Alamein in October 1942. A number of the bodies were brought in from other burial sites across the Western Desert and reburied there in 1943. My great-uncle had been serving in the 22nd Motor Battalion of the New Zealand Infantry when he was killed in the Western Desert on 24 October 1942. He was just 21 years old – the same age I was when I joined the regiment.

I was the first member of our family to visit his grave, and it was a powerful moment for me. There was just something about being there that was really special. No one else was at the cemetery – just me and the WODF. I paid my respects to my great-uncle, then took out a piece of paper and a pencil, and made a rubbing of his plaque so I could send it to his close family.

Then the WODF and I walked around and looked at the other graves. There were three rows where all of the guys had been killed together in tanks or artillery units. They'd been buried there together as a group.

It was all so clean and so well looked after, despite being right up against the desert.

And, as we started walking back, two doves flew past us, then out to the entrance.

*

When we flew into Dubai, where Lieutenant General Mateparae was to meet his Emirati counterpart, we were picked up at the hotel by these two black Mercedes S200s. The drivers were in full local dress, and once the Chief of Defence Force and I got into our car we discovered that neither seatbelts nor the speed limit existed to them. As the person tasked with assessing potential threats, I had to have a chat with them about that!

When we got to the Emiratis' officers mess, we saw that it was very elaborate. Easily the most extravagant meal I'd ever had in my life. The food just kept coming, and I had more knives and forks to negotiate than I could ever imagine I needed. Way more than we'd been taught how to use in the etiquette section of our training course! That meal just went on and on and on until we were pretty much rolling out the door.

The last part of the Chief of Defence Force's trip involved meeting the crew of HMNZS *Te Kaha* at Abu Dhabi. We drove out there in the Mercedes with our drivers, and boarded the ship for the arrival formalities, before heading to the officers' mess to socialise.

8

FAMILIAR TERRITORY

MY NEXT OVERSEAS TRIP was in April 2009, and it took me back into slightly more familiar territory, as I was part of the close protection team accompanying the then-Minister of Foreign Affairs and Trade, Murray McCully, to Afghanistan.

Before the minister was due to arrive in Afghanistan, we spent a week doing prep in New Zealand, then another a week and a half in country. There, we checked out all of his meeting venues, the routes we'd take him on and the hotel where he'd be staying. We needed to stay low-profile the whole time, so I made sure we had vehicles that wouldn't draw attention in the traffic. The only vehicle that we would clean up, I decided, would be the VIP's; if we had a number of matching clean vehicles, we'd stick out a bit. My reasoning was that our lives were more precious than having clean cars.

Minister McCully was travelling with an advisor, the defence attaché, the head of the New Zealand embassy in Kabul and a private secretary. After he arrived in Afghanistan, we took him around Kabul, where he met with President Karzai and some of his ministers. Then we headed up to Bamyan to visit the 131 New Zealand troops based there as part of the Provincial Reconstruction Team (PRT). We got to spend Anzac Day with them, which was pretty special. While we were there, we also saw what was left of the two huge sixth-century Buddha statues that were blown up by the Taliban back in 2001. The PRT had done a really good job up there. It was the first province to be handed back to its citizens, and that alone was proof of how well they'd worked with the locals. Kiwis have probably done more peacekeeping than combat operations over the years, and therefore we are really good at influencing hearts and minds. We're really good in the peacekeeping environment.

Back in Kabul, we stayed at the Serena Hotel, which was quite flash and catered for Westerners. It was very well protected, but had been attacked a couple of times, including once in January the year before – and in that attack, at least six people were killed. So we knew we had to have a really good plan there. We booked out an entire floor, and ensured we had the weapons and ammunition to hold it for a long time should anything happen. There was no way anyone was going to get onto our floor – they could have tried, but they would have found themselves in a hell of a fight.

*

Once he'd finished all his visits, the minister asked to sit down with me one on one. Outside of his diplomatic visits while we were in country, the minister had also been taking care of another task: he'd been fact-finding to see whether the government should redeploy the regiment to Afghanistan in some capacity. This time the International Security Assistance Force (ISAF) wanted us to be in Kabul instead of out doing long-range reconnaissance work.

The ISAF was a NATO-led coalition, and had been established to oversee the training of the Afghan National Security Forces, including their police and army. All of the special forces operating in Afghanistan – the British SAS, US Special Forces, the Australian SAS – were training the country's internal forces to become competent at securing their own backyard.

He was keen to know what I thought – and what the boys in the regiment would think – about going back to Afghanistan. 'I've talked to everyone else,' he told me. 'The CO, the Prime Minister, everyone around me. But I want to know what you think the boys want to do? Do they want to be here?'

'Yeah, of course,' I replied.

'It could be for a long period of time …' he added, and I just nodded. Everyone wanted to be there. Then he said, 'Tell me what you think you'd be doing.'

'High-risk arrests of high-value targets,' I replied. 'And

training and enabling local security forces like the other ISAF units are doing.'

I knew this lined up with what the CO would have already told him, but it was also exactly what I knew all of the boys wanted to do.

He asked me some more questions, and I could tell he was really listening to what I had to say. He wanted to know what we wanted, and he was turning to me as a representative of the boys. Ultimately, as we'd be the ones executing orders, this showed me that he was prepared to fully do his homework. Although, it would have been interesting to see what would have had happened if I'd said I didn't think the boys were keen!

*

On the way back from Afghanistan, the team and I flew via Australia into Papua New Guinea, where we spent four weeks conducting jungle training with the rest of the squadron. Then I headed home to New Zealand. And it wasn't long after I got back that we started to get wind that the unit was going to deploy back to Afghanistan.

Then, in August, Murray McCully told parliament:

Above all other considerations, the Government decided that a further deployment of the SAS to Afghanistan was in the best interests of New Zealand and New Zealanders. New Zealanders are a highly mobile people. New Zealand nationals travel in planes, and they stay in hotel rooms and resorts. Where terrorists strike around the world, the chances are that New Zealanders will be at risk. All New Zealanders today have a strong interest in reducing the threat of international terrorism and the ability of Afghanistan to play host to the terrorist groups that are present there.

And the following month, about 70 of us were deployed on Operation Wātea, Rotation 1, to support the Crisis Response Unit (CRU) operations and training, although we could be deployed as a unilateral force if required.

The CRU was one of three Tier One National Mission Units (NMUs) working under the General Directorate of Police Special Units (GDPSU), and governed by the Ministry of Interior. Three units sat under the GDPSU: Task Force 222 (the CRU, located in Kabul), Task Force 333 (Commandos, located in Loghar Province), and Task Force 444 (Afghan Territorial Force, based in Helmand Province). All three units were mandated to conduct high-risk arrests, counterterrorism and counter-narcotics operations. The CRU's specific responsibilities were the security of Kabul, and acting as the first-responder unit to high-profile attacks that threatened the capital. The other two NMUs covered a broader geographical area, and conducted a variety of reconnaissance and high-risk arrest operations.

This time round, we were based on the outskirts of Kabul. Most of the squadron was at Camp Warehouse, which was directly opposite Kabul Military Training Center (KMTC), out to the east of the city. It was a French camp, but as well as the French and ourselves, there were also a couple of Bulgarian officers and a Georgian unit providing camp security there, too. The best thing about it was that the food was really good. And they had wine, which a lot of other bases didn't have. The Europeans wouldn't have known how to do without it!

As for me, I spent most of the deployment based at the CRU's Camp Olympus, which was about 13 kilometres away from Camp Warehouse and close to the centre of Kabul. It was right next to Ghazi Stadium, which was home to the Afghan national football team and the Afghan women's national football team. I was part of an eight-man training team, and I was Training Second in Command. The Oracle was also there as the Training Team Commander.

Our goal was to get the CRU up to speed, so that they'd be able to protect their country from once again falling into the hands of the Taliban or other terrorist groups. They had come in as police, then gone through a selection process to join the CRU. A civilian security company called DynCorp took them through the basic special police training, then we took them through advanced skills.

The CRU consisted of four squadrons: A, B, C and D. The three strike squadrons – A, B and C – rotated one at a time through a remote training camp at Surobi, which was out to the east of Kabul. It was an isolated camp quite a distance from everyone else, and most of the training team was out there. Meanwhile, D Squadron – the standalone covert surveillance team – was at Camp Olympus with me and one other trainer. We had to build up their capability to do covert surveillance on the streets, which meant I'd gone from doing long-range at-distance operations to close-range ones.

The squadron consisted of men and women, which was interesting because culturally men are dominant in Afghanistan. This cultural nuance provided me with some challenges, and I decided that I would spend more time with the woman, if required, to bring them up to par with their male counterparts.

The first thing we did with them was simply watch and learn. For a few years before we arrived, the Norwegians had already been here and had done a lot of work with the CRU, so it was a matter of figuring out what they still needed. We walked around or sat in our observation post just by our sleeping quarters, and got to know the squadron commanders, talked to the Camp CO, and spent a lot of time chatting and drinking tea, doing our best to figure it all out while also being non-threatening and slowly gaining the CRU's trust. To build trust we had to show that we were up to the task. One question I got asked a few times was whether I'd done combat operations in Afghanistan before. 'Yeah,' I'd reply. 'Long-range patrols, but not in the city.' That seemed to earn me a bit of respect, at least.

We also observed the CRU during training and on operations, and then we designed our programmes and presented them. We asked the CRU for their feedback, and made sure they were happy with everything before beginning. It was only after we'd done all this that we got into the actual training.

And, once we finally got out into the field and they saw what we could do, they fully trusted that we knew what we were doing.

*

As part of the training role, I was expected to interface at quite a high level with people like the CO of the CRU and, at times, the Minister of Interior. Before one of my first meetings, I decided I needed to talk to the Oracle. I wanted to check to see if I was lining up with his intent.

I called him, and he just said to me, 'Jamie, what do you think you should do?' I spoke in general terms about what I should be talking about in these meetings, and he said, 'Yep, that's the right answer. Talk to you later.' And then he hung up.

It was an echo of the question my mum had asked me all those years ago, when I was tossing up whether to join the army or not. It was also a vote of confidence from the Oracle: he was basically letting me know he believed I could handle those meetings.

I definitely benefited from having him to call on, even if he was at a different camp. Until then, I had thought that to be a good leader you had to be quite prescriptive and keep people in a particular lane. But the Oracle wasn't like that at all. His mentoring skills had been honed over many years of doing a broad scope of work, and he was great at remote leadership and letting people learn for themselves. He would give us his intent, then tell us to make the decisions. He'd suggest ways of doing things, but ultimately leave the steps along the path up to us.

It didn't take long before I started to feel at home at Camp Olympus. There were about 280 CRU members, and they had it pretty bad when we turned up. Their barrack block was just a bunch of shipping containers stacked on top of each other. It was also the middle of winter and snowing outside, and for heating they had a heated coil but no grille, so it was really unsafe. I could hear rats running up the sides of the containers and around inside them, and there was rubbish and crap everywhere. The hygiene was terrible. They had a septic tank that always blew, and the toilets and showers were horrendous.

We got one Portacom, then another one, then we built a concrete pad and got a third one. We had a kitchen and two accommodation blocks sorted. We just kept building and improving things all the time, including introducing heat pumps.

When Willie and I were there together for a bit, we decided at one point enough was enough with the bathroom situation. We grabbed some bleach and cleaned one toilet and one shower, then put a notice on the wall in Pashtu: *This is for the CRU instructors. Do not use.* Do you think they took any notice? Of course not. They just laughed, and were happy to have a clean toilet and shower to use.

We regularly ate with the CRU guys in their camp. In the mornings, a ute loaded with raw goat meat would turn up, and it would be surrounded by flies and wasps. They'd then cook it in these massive pots, and we'd go join them for a good feed. As long as they cooked it thoroughly, I didn't really give a toss about how it arrived. But, during the time we were there, everyone in the team got sick except for me, the Oracle and Willie.

Slowly, the Americans injected money into Camp Olympus, and sorted out the CRU's accommodation and got them weapons and proper vehicles. That helped to build up the CRU's capability and effectiveness.

*

For us, building and maintaining relationships was important. It was all about hearts and minds. We didn't want to tell people what to do. But it took time to find the right footing for that approach. My biggest issue was that I had really high standards and expectations, because that's the environment I'd come from. I was in charge of D squadron's covert surveillance programme, and to begin with I ran the training as if I was delivering it to SAS soldiers. Soon, though, I realised the CRU members didn't have anything like the same educational background and motivation as we did, so they took longer to take new and advanced information on board. And none of this was helped by the fact only 80 per cent of what my interpreter was saying both ways was accurate due to translation competency. It took me about four months to adjust my expectations and become more fluid, so that I could get them to a basic level that the next tour could work off. It was a long game.

One challenge I faced was a somewhat loose approach to turning up to training. At the start, we trained them to shoot and move, then started scaffolding the training to more advanced skills, and then surveillance techniques. The women in the squadron were always at training and keen to learn, which I respected in comparison to the men.

In fact, the women in the squadron were the standouts in the group. They didn't moan. They just turned up and did the work. And their shooting was good. They initially had these cheap Russian or Chinese pistols and ammunition, but they still managed to hit targets really accurately. As soon as we gave them proper pistols they were all over it. I put their tenacity down to their upbringing. They were a hell of a lot more resilient than the men. You could throw anything at the women, and they'd get on with it.

The men, however, had a different approach to training. They weren't nearly so committed about being there. I expected there to be the same number of people in the room in the afternoon as there had been in the morning, but this wasn't often the case. Between sessions, some of the men would just walk out the gate and go home – and not come back till the next day.

I knew I had to do something, but what? I decided to introduce an attendance requirement of nine days every two weeks. They'd also have to be on the last exercise to make sure I could confirm they'd learnt the skills. Then I organised a graduation ceremony. It was held in the gymnasium at the end of the two-week course, and I created certificates to make things official, which I knew they really liked.

Everyone turned up to the graduation.

This is going to be interesting, I thought.

One by one, the names of the people who had passed the course were called out, and they'd come up, shake my hand and be presented with their certificate, then everyone would clap.

Then we got to the end of the list, and there was still a bunch of guys sitting there with no certificates. They started looking round, confused.

'OK, that's it, guys,' I said. 'You can come back and try again at the next course ...'

A bit of a ruckus broke out. 'Give me the certificate! I was here!' they were shouting, and some of them had to be held back by their mates.

'You weren't there, mate,' I replied. 'You were here for like, three days,' I said to one, then to another, 'Where were you?' and to a third, 'I saw you walk out the gate. I asked you where you were going and you said you were going home.'

This one guy just kept kicking off and insisting he should get his certificate. He just kept going on and on, and then he challenged me to a fight. In the end, I agreed. If I hadn't, it would have festered. He needed to be able to save face. 'All right,' I said. 'If you want to fight, then I'm happy to do that. We'll do it here in the gym. I'll bring one person. You bring one person. We'll have a fight. Whoever wins, the other person shuts their mouth. I'll meet you back here in ten minutes.'

At the allotted time, I went back to the gym, and there was no one there.

*

That was the first of a handful of times that I was challenged to a fight.

They're big on taekwondo over there, so they had a big mat, a couple of bags and some weights in the gym. It meant I was able to keep up with my training while I was away. Some of the locals saw me kicking and punching the bag, and may have thought I was handy. I had been doing a bit of Brazilian jiu-jitsu for a couple of years at that point, and I'd also been doing some mixed martial arts (MMA).

Then one day while I was training, two guys walked in. One had his 12-ounce boxing gloves on and went and stood on the other side of the mat. The other came and tapped me on the shoulder. 'Hey,' he said, 'my friend wants to fight you.'

'What do you mean?' I'd already been there an hour, and I was just using bag gloves – small and very thin gloves to protect the hands when hitting a punching bag.

'My friend wants to fight you,' this guy reiterated.

'Mate, I've just finished a full-on session. Why would I want to fight him? And why does he want to fight me?'

'He just does. You want to fight?'

I thought about it, then I said, 'OK, fine. But I've only got these gloves. Here, give him one and see if he's still keen.'

He was. I thought, *Oh, right. We're going to play this game, are we?* It was clear we were going to have a proper fight.

I got on the mat and said, 'OK, what are the rules?'

'Boxing,' the guy's mate said.

'No, no,' I said. 'If he wants a fight, the rules are MMA rules. That means elbows, knees, punches. We can take each other to the ground. Does he do wrestling?'

133

'Yeah, he does.'

'Oh, cool. Sweet. I do Brazilian jiu-jitsu, so it should be even then. He OK?'

Both guys nodded.

We got into it, and he started boxing away, then I took him down to the ground and started punching him in the face. He was quite strong and, as he was a wrestler, he ended up getting me on my back. *Here we go!* I thought. I managed to get onto my feet, and I kicked him off into the corner. But when I went in to punch him, he did the splits and I punched right over the top of him into nothing. Then I grabbed him and put him in a front choke, and he tapped out. That brought the fight to an end.

Afterwards, his mate came over and said to me, 'He wants to fight you again.'

'Nah, mate, that's it,' I said. 'The fight's over. I won. Now get out!'

The pair of them shuffled out the door and away they went.

*

My second fight was against their taekwondo champion. He was only a little guy, but he was pretty good. I'd seen him do flying, spinning kicks on elevated clay pots.

We started out having a sparring session that turned into a real fight with half the CRU in the gymnasium watching it. He was doing all these fancy kicks, so I decided I wasn't going to muck around, and I just brawled it. He kept running away and everyone would laugh, and he'd laugh as well. At one point, I even kicked him up the arse as he was running away.

I reckon these guys wanted to challenge me because they were trying to gauge how good they were compared with Westerners. They only got to fight among themselves otherwise.

As well as those one-on-one fights, we used to have what we called 'King of the Mat' challenges. At the end of our hand-to-hand combat sessions, it would be two instructors against all of them. They'd all go hard-out against the two of us. It was their opportunity to release some energy, and provided an outlet for their frustrations. For us, it was the same. We weren't trying to fight each other properly. It was just a good activity to end the session.

*

D squadron deployed on their first target-reconnaissance job about halfway through our tour. A couple of the CRU women did a walk-by first, but they couldn't get close enough. I was sitting in a Toyota Corolla down the road with two other CRU guys and an interpreter. We needed to get the information back to HQ fast, as the target was time sensitive, and also the area would soon be crowded with people coming back from work. That meant we had to execute the operation quickly that evening. I thought about doing it, but I wasn't sure I'd be able to without drawing attention to us, being a foreigner. I was wearing cargo pants, a green snug-pack jacket and a beanie, and carried a short (pistol) and a long (rifle), and had a small breakaway bag with extra ammunition and medical gear just in case.

One of the CRU team said, 'No, you should be all right.'

'You reckon?'

'Yeah, you just look like a Russian Afghani.'

Out on the street, everyone was wearing cargo pants and fly jackets, with the pockets full of stuff. They all looked militant, too.

'Are you sure?' I said. 'What about those kids playing soccer in that alleyway?

'Don't worry about them.'

'Are you sure, man? Because if they ping us, it's on. What if they run up there and knock on the door?'

'No, we'll be right.'

We had a few guys in another Corolla just down the street as the Quick Reaction Force (QRF). It was in an area where there were all these interconnecting compounds and narrow alleyways. It would have been easy to get caught up in there. We got out of the car and started walking, and as we walked through these kids I wondered, *How's this going to go?* Then one of the boys called out, 'Salaam aleikum!' So the interpreter stopped and chatted to him for a bit, then we carried on walking and got the information we needed before leaving. When we got out the other side, I asked what the kid had said.

'Look at the two uncles walking through here,' replied the interpreter.

They hadn't clocked me at all.

9
HIGH ALERT

WHENEVER WE WEREN'T TRAINING at Camp Olympus, we'd be sitting there watching what was going on. We had to react when the CRU reacted. They'd either get Immediate Action tasks – where they would respond immediately to something that had happened in Kabul – or they'd deliberately plan for and then execute a high-risk arrest. Initially, they wouldn't always tell us when they were leaving on missions. We'd just see them start to gear up or drive out the gate!

This could happen at any time of the day or night, so we were constantly on alert. We had to be ready to gear up at all times, so that we could follow the CRU out the gate. When that happened, we'd find out what was going on as we were on the way. There'd be a couple of us in the vehicle, and one of the other guys would go in and see the CO or the operations officer. They'd find out what was happening, and give a reference as to which police district things were happening in. That intel would then be fed to us as we went.

The CRU had their lines of communications where they'd get their intelligence from. It would go through the various channels up to the Ministry of the Interior, who would then delegate it to whatever units needed to do the job. The main groups that were active in Kabul at the time were the Taliban, the Haqqani network and the Hezb-e-Islami Gulbuddin (HIG). These groups functioned because they had money, weapons, explosives, ammunition and suicide vests arranged within a network. They'd decentralise these component parts to make it harder for us to shut down their operations. Our operations therefore focused on identifying these networks and hitting them simultaneously, sometimes with other ISAF or special forces partners if required. Any high-value targets (HVTs) part of the operation were processed through the Afghan legal process, so we took lawyers with us on most operations to ensure Afghan rule of law was followed. This protected both us and the CRU, and developed the CRU as an effective, ethical and trusted Special Police Unit.

The terrorist groups in Afghanistan were funded by sophisticated financial networks, including donations from non-state actors and Taliban taxation systems focusing on opium cultivation and supply and other goods. This funding enabled these groups to buy relatively cheap weapons, explosives and equipment required to fight the war. In

Afghanistan you could buy an AK-47 for roughly US$500 with low-cost ammunition to match. That made it a cheap war for them, but it wasn't a cheap war for the coalition forces, who required the latest technology to track them down and destroy them while protecting their troops on the ground. But each time we took stuff out of circulation, we could work out how many lives we'd saved, because the Americans came up with an equation that assigned a value to individual items. A suicide vest would equal maybe five lives. A 105-millimetre shell would equal maybe a platoon.

During the Afghan war, the Haqqani network, led by Jalaluddin Haqqani, operated in eastern Afghanistan and across the border in northwest Pakistan, and had ties with Al-Qaeda and the Taliban. Having a base of operations across the border made it easier for them to plan and prepare cross-border operations. When they crossed over, we would track them into the country and try to target them just before they bedded down. They'd come across the border, come into the city, stay a few nights, then at the time planned, execute their attack. A few of these groups got caught before they managed to carry out their attacks, so they changed their tactics and started to come across the border and execute the attack quickly, or they'd cross and go into a complete comms blackout. That made it really hard to track them. Usually, they'd come in and talk back to Pakistan, which gave us a chance to ping them.

*

In October 2009, we had some intelligence through our headquarters that there was a Haqqani group that was going to come across the border from Pakistan and do an operation. That usually meant killing a lot of people in an initial assault at a significant point in the city, barricading themselves within that significant point, engaging in combat with the Afghan National Security Forces (ANSF), then blowing themselves up as soon as the ANSF got close in a bid to take as many people as possible with them. The intent being – as with all terrorist groups – to gain media attention, to validate their existence to their benefactors and promote themselves to get additional funding, and to recruit new members.

We had got word that this group was coming in, and they were being tracked. Then their comms went silent. At that point, we didn't have intelligence to do a high-risk arrest.

Then, in the early hours of the morning of 28 October, about five of them turned up at the Bakhtar private guest house in Kabul. They didn't raise suspicions, as they were wearing police uniforms, but then they shot and killed the guest house's two security guards and opened fire on the guest house using rifle grenades and a machine gun.

They managed to get through over the gate, before being held at bay by a couple of UN security guards – among the guests were 25 UN staff. This allowed most of the hotel's guests to evacuate from the building and get to the safety of a separate laundry room at the back of the property.

One of the Haqqani operatives became a human Claymore mine. He had a bunch of ball bearings inside plastic explosive strapped to his stomach. Once the guards were shot, he went in first and moved into the courtyard in front of the building, where the vehicles were parked. Once there, he detonated himself and killed two UN workers preparing a vehicle to head out for the day. They didn't stand a chance. The explosion was of such a huge velocity that the ball bearings went straight through the glass of an armoured Land Cruiser sitting in the carpark. This first explosion cleared the way for the second wave of the attack.

The next two attackers also wore suicide vests, and between them they must have had more than 10 kilograms of explosives. They clearly knew the layout of the building, as one headed downstairs to the kitchen and dining room, while the other went upstairs towards the bedrooms. When they detonated themselves, they killed all but one person in the dining area.

The CRU had headed out pretty quick, but there was a lag in our arrival time due to gathering information on the situation from our HQ. And then the city was gridlocked due to the cordons in place. By the time Willie and I arrived, the CRU was already there and all of the attackers were dead. The place was on fire, and there was a big plume of black smoke over the middle of the city. As well as the two security guards, five UN employees and an Afghan citizen had been killed.

Willie and I sat outside for a while, providing cover while the fire was extinguished. Then, once the flames were out, we were able to go into the courtyard. As soon as we walked in, we saw the first attacker lying dead on the ground with his guts blown out. We then saw the bodies of the two dead UN workers by their vehicle. They were both quite young – in their twenties maybe. *Your poor families, they don't even know you're dead*, I thought. I felt sorry for them, but I also had a mission to complete. Then the only woman who'd survived from the kitchen was brought out, along with about five bodies from the breakfast area, which they lined up in the courtyard. The woman who'd survived was in shock already, but when she saw the bodies of her friends she just started screaming and crying. It was pretty confronting for her and she was very distressed.

Once the fire went down, Willie and I took two groups of CRU into the building. Willie started clearing from the third floor up, and I started on the ground floor. There was a lot of water coming in from the top because the fire fighters were still hosing things down.

When I went back outside, a British guy on the cordon called me over. 'Some of my friends are trapped in a safe room in that building,' he said, then handed me his phone so I could talk to them. 'We're in the bunker,' said the guy on the phone. 'It's really hot. I can see smoke coming under the door.'

They must be in the building somewhere, I thought, *but where?* I couldn't work it out, and the guy on the phone couldn't tell me either. So we went back inside, down into where the fire damage was extensive, trying to find the safe room. It was still burning and there were embers, so we probably shouldn't have been down there, but we had a job to do.

'Where are you?' I kept saying to the guy on the phone. 'Tell me where you are. Tell me what you can see so we can find you. Where are you?'

He just kept saying, 'We're in the guesthouse. We can feel the heat of the flames. We're going to die!'

'*Where* in the guesthouse? Where are you in relation to the kitchen?'

'I don't know.'

'As soon as you tell me where you are, I'll come and get you right away.'

But he couldn't tell me. He just talked around where they were, and never told me anything concrete. In the end, I was completely over it. 'Listen, man,' I said. 'If you can't tell me where you are, I can't help you. The fire is out and the area's secure, so just come out.' Then I gave the phone back to his mate and said, 'If he tells you exactly where they are, we can go and get them right away. But I've got to go now.' We had to move at that point because the CRU were reorganising themselves to head back to Camp Olympus to prepare themselves for further attacks in the city.

You would have thought that someone who wanted to be rescued would have been able to tell you exactly how they'd got to where they were. Not this guy. We didn't end up finding him at all – but that was because he was in a building next door! I think he was just overwhelmed, but the good news is that he and the others he was with were all OK.

*

The use of suicide vests always added another layer of complexity to any operation, as it meant we had to be very careful when assaulting or moving through a particular area. It was always pretty confronting in situations where people were prepared to blow themselves up and take you with them. We were very methodical in our work, and made sure we didn't run to our deaths.

The only way you can counter people who are so invested in what they're doing that they'll blow themselves up is through changing the ideology. You've got to identify where they're being enticed or coerced into that ideology, and you've got to counter it with facts and evidence. You've got to give them a reason why they shouldn't be doing it, which can be very difficult if a member of their family has been killed or they've lost their home.

Everyone plays a part in countering the ideology: the soldiers on the ground shooting the terrorists with the weapons; the counter-ideology teams on social media; the people in the community working alongside marginalised young people to prevent them from going down that path; and the higher-level intelligence community conducting operations as close to assets as possible, and getting the information to target the people who are funding operations. There's a lot to it and everyone has to have their hand in to minimise the effect.

Our next big operation was the suicide attacks on Pashtunistan Square that took place on 18 January 2010 – the ones during which Willie and I were photographed by a French journalist. But not all of our actions were in the city. There were also occasions when we were called on to do operations in the nearby provinces. One involved going out to a rural area in search of an HVT who had been responsible for the deaths of a number of members of the coalition forces and the local population. It was an ISAF Special Operations Forces (SOF) combined operation executed across three target areas – one in the city, and two in a mountainous area bordering Kabul – with the overall objective of taking out a network. The British SAS and US special forces with us and our partnered Afghan Forces needed to hit each target all at the same time. In other words, we all had to make entry on each target simultaneously.

The lawyers who came along with us always turned up wearing suits and carrying briefcases, and they wanted to know where they were going, but we couldn't tell them that night. Operational security meant not giving away any operational information that could compromise things. If we did, there was always the risk the targets would be informed. So the lawyers got into the helicopters with us, then climbed out onto a mountain range. The helicopters took off, and these guys were just standing there, in the middle of the night, with their briefcases and their suits and their good shoes up in the mountains.

'You guys just stick with me,' I said, and we set off.

During any operation we would have a number of aircraft overhead, and an Intelligence, Surveillance and Reconnaissance (ISR) aircraft scanning around and ahead of us with thermal technology to pick up any threats as we moved. They also sent down infrared light so we had way points to follow. They pretty much mapped the whole walk for us. It took us a couple of hours to make our way 7 kilometres over the mountain range and get to the HVT's compound, but we arrived in time for H hour.

I ended up leading that assault into the compound because the CRU was still in its infancy, and we had to also demonstrate to them that we could be trusted by leading rather than bringing up the rear. We put in our marksmen first, then led the CRU in. We moved in slowly and quietly without the residents of the compound even knowing. Dogs were going off all around us, but for some reason no one got up to find out what was going on. I don't think they believed we'd ever be able to get in.

We walked right into the HVT's bedroom while he was asleep, took the AK-47 sitting beside his bed, and put him in the bag – cuffed with blindfold and ear muffs. Then we searched his compound, called the helicopters on, and he got taken off from there.

This particular HVT went through the judicial process, and unfortunately the prosecutors didn't have all the evidence lined up, so he got out and went back into play. The judicial process is such that warrants are executed on viable intelligence, and unfortunately in this case due diligence was not followed. This was a big lesson for us, and we made sure from that point to have enough evidence to prosecute. It was very frustrating to get so close to getting him into jail ... and then see him walk free.

*

Every time the CRU went out, we went out, regardless of whether it was for something small or big. There was a lot of up and down, standing to and standing down. I drove myself pretty hard over those seven months, but we were gaining traction, so it was worth it.

Early on in the piece, the Oracle told me to chill out and take a rest, but I didn't take any notice. He could see what was happening even when I couldn't. And, true to his leadership style, he must have figured I was going to have to find out the hard way myself. I did. I hit the wall.

When you're over there, you're working seven days a week, 24 hours a day. We had Sundays off, but it wasn't really a day off. We were in the middle of the city, and we still had to worry about security. We were in camp with the CRU, and they were friendly, but you never knew if someone wasn't happy with what you'd said to them a few days earlier and wanted to do something about it. There were enough examples of green-on-blue attacks happening across Afghanistan, where ANSF members had killed coalition-force soldiers inside secure camps.

We were always carrying pistols to protect ourselves in camp because of this possibility, but also in case the camp was attacked, and therefore I was on high alert all the time. I didn't really sleep through any of those tours – I don't think anyone does. Your brain is just registering threats all the time, so that you can make sure you're on your game when you need to be. You couldn't let your guard down, because if you did someone could take advantage of it.

Part of the reason I'd worked myself into the ground was the same reason I was there: because I had a high tolerance for stress, and high expectations of myself. And people had high expectations of me. This is a normal part of being in a tier-one special forces unit. But there is the negative side of being driven by that idea of always going a little bit further.

It all starts on the selection course. One foot in front of the other, no matter what. Lean in. It doesn't matter how much storm there is, or how much weight is on your back. You just keep going. That's it – you just keep doing that the whole time. It has to be that way because you have to be able to operate in small groups or by yourself behind enemy lines. You have to have high stress tolerance, resilience and grit – but it takes its toll.

By the time I got to month five, after constantly training the CRU and heading out on operations in the city and outlying provinces, I went to the Oracle and said that I'd realised he was right. I'd started exhibiting physical signs of burnout, significant fatigue and notably, ulcers had formed around the retina in one of my eyes. It was time to take a short break.

'Take a week,' the Oracle said.

'What about D squadron?' I replied.

'Don't worry about them. They'll just carry on with their job.'

So I just chilled at Camp Olympus for a week, and it was the best thing I could have done. I stepped back from the day-to-day stuff for a bit. I read a book and tried to get my head out of the weeds.

*

When I got home after that seven-month stint in Afghanistan, I started contemplating leaving the regiment. I took myself there, but it had bled a lot out of me.

I found myself feeling very insecure in my house back in Papakura. There were times when I would wake up suddenly to gunshots going off outside my window. Looking outside, I'd realise the shots weren't real – they were being created by my brain – but I'd still go around repeatedly checking all the doors to make sure they were locked. I kept having to remind myself I wasn't in Afghanistan anymore. I was in New Zealand, and there weren't terrorists running around trying to get me. At one point, I even considered buying a shotgun and keeping it under my bed, but I knew that was crazy so I managed to convince myself not to go down that track.

We did have psych debriefs when we got home, and the support we needed was available, but that didn't necessarily mean we used it. It was a case of bringing the horse to water: if I'd been directed to have more sessions with psychs I would have, but I wasn't, so I didn't. I think it was a matter of everyone leading everyone else to believe they were fine. In that sort of environment, where you're competing against your peers, you put on a brave face and pretend everything's good so that your career won't suffer. At that time, there was still some work to be done around handling the transition time between an operation and coming home. It has to be very carefully crafted based on what the specific group of soldiers have been through, and it needs to be required – not simply offered.

Over time, and possibly thanks to some of the stuff I'd been told by the psychs, I began to figure out how to identify and question the way I was feeling. It took a while, but as I got more aware of my thoughts, and more able to question them, it helped me depower the sense of paranoia. I didn't always know what to do about those dark thoughts I was having, but I did try to sit on them, and give myself time to figure it all out. One thing that I found really helped was dialling back some of the stuff I did outside of work – so, not skydiving all weekend!

*

Operation Wātea had initially been slated to end in March 2011, but it got extended for another year. After the first three rotations, the troop number was cut from 75 down to about 45, and the length of each deployment for special forces soldiers was also cut back to four months due to the high operational tempo. By this time, the trained state of the CRU was better than when we'd started, so we only needed a small group to enable them to conduct their operations.

After a little over a year at home, I was on my way back to Afghanistan. This time, instead of training CRU members, our role was to enable them to do their operations. Much the same as when I'd been there in 2009, we reacted whenever the CRU reacted. There were ten of us – four mentors and a handful of guys with specific capabilities, to support CRU operations. The mentors were based at Camp Olympus, but the rest of us were at Camp Warehouse. Since we had a smaller group this time round, we had to one-up our positions. So, while in 2009 I'd been a troop sergeant, this time I became a troop/ground commander. It was a really good opportunity for me to sink my teeth into as a leader.

The CRU team was happy to see us again and they certainly hadn't forgotten me. They had become a lot cheekier, too. On one job, everyone was busy preparing to head out on an operation with the vehicles all lined up and ready, when all of a sudden I heard one of the CRU guys yell out, 'Jaaaamieee! Ladies commander!' They were taking the piss out of me because I had trained the women on the previous tour. After that, a voice would call out every now and then, 'Ladies commander!' and they'd all laugh. They were always respectful about it, and I liked that they had the confidence to have a bit of banter with me.

It showed they felt comfortable with me, and that was the relationship-building long game right there. It all trickles back. I knew that as soon as I wanted them to do something, they'd do it. I was able to just sit there in the background and let them do what they needed to.

Two months deep, things had been pretty uneventful. The SAS boys were starting to get a little bit ratty, and to counter the thumb-twiddling we had to make sure their training was creative. And I kept reminding them, they didn't know what was round the corner. 'The last month could be crazy,' I said. 'We just don't know.'

10

THE BIG ONE

ON 22 JUNE, PRESIDENT Barack Obama made a speech to announce that 10,000 US troops would leave Afghanistan by the end of the year. And, just six days later, one of the signallers came and woke me up at about 10.30pm. 'You need to come over to the ops room,' he said. 'Something's happening in the city.'

I put on my jandals and walked over.

At the back of the room stood the senior national officer (SNO), who was responsible for making decisions about our operations countrywide. He was watching the three screens that had the news going and the ISR coverage of the target. We knew that what the news was reporting wasn't necessarily accurate, but we were more interested in what we could see than what they were saying. The ISR platform overhead showed us thermal signatures, and there were a lot of comms going back and forth.

'What's going on?' I asked the SNO.

'The Intercontinental Hotel's been taken over.'

The Intercontinental? That was the luxury hotel I'd stayed at back in December 2002, when we provided the security detail for the Minister of Foreign Affairs. On this night in 2011, there was a range of people staying there, including foreign businesspeople and diplomats who were there to attend various high-level events both inside the hotel and in Kabul. There was also a wedding taking place in one of the function rooms. Like the other hotels in the city, the Intercontinental had always been seen as quite safe, as it always had strong security, but on the TV screens before me now I could see the terrorists up on the roof shooting down to the ground, where the ANSF were in a cordon position surrounding the building itself. Believe it or not, this sort of gun battle wasn't especially unusual or worrying. The worrying part was the fact that a lot of the rounds and rockets the terrorists were firing from the roof were landing in the surrounding neighbourhood, meaning the lives of innocent people and their families were in danger.

'Who have we got down there?' I asked.

'Two of the mentors and their squadrons.'

'So sixty to eighty people?'

'Yeah,' said the SNO. 'I want you to go down there, too.'

I wasn't sure. 'There's a few blokes there already,' I said. 'They should have the numbers to resolve the situation?'

'The problem is, the threat group keeps coming out of one of the rooms,' he replied, 'so we don't accurately know how many of them there are.'

It was a 20-minute trip just to get to the hotel, and I caught myself thinking, *I don't want to waste my time going all the way down there only to find out it's already over.* I thought everything would probably be resolved before I even arrived.

'Are you *sure* you want me to go down?' I said.

'Yeah,' said the SNO. 'Go down.'

So I went and woke everyone up, gave them the brief, then went back to the SNO one more time and told him, 'We're ready.'

'Yep. Off you go.'

*

In Kabul there was a curfew at night, so the roads were clear and it felt like driving on a racetrack. The only thing we had to slow down for was the police checkpoints, but after we'd showed them our ID we just went for it. While we were driving down, one of our Task Force mentors called me to say they were in the lobby of the hotel with the CRU, and were waiting for us to arrive before they started clearing. I reported this to the rest of the team and – with renewed enthusiasm because we were going to get involved – we moved quickly to get down there.

We stopped when we got to the outer cordon, which was about 300 metres from the hotel entry, as driving up the road would have exposed us and we could have got shot at. A security party stayed with the vehicles, while the rest of us moved up on foot to the hotel at pace, with Steve at the front as the lead assaulter. When we got to the incident control point, we found the Minister of Interior, the CO of the CRU and the COs of the other units on site waiting for us.

'Is it clear up the road to the hotel?' I asked the CO of the CRU.

'Yeah, but some of the guards are a bit jittery.'

'They're not going to shoot, are they?'

He smiled. 'I don't know.'

'Well,' I said, 'your guys can go first then!'

We started walking up the driveway, and a few shots cracked off. Then, as we drew closer, it kicked off big time. There was quite a significant two-way gun battle into and out of the hotel. News reports at the time said that the terrorists had come up the main road and just shot their way through the checkpoints, then went into the Intercontinental, but that's not actually what happened. The hotel was at the bottom of a small hill that had a security outpost on top of it. They killed the two ANP guys up there, then just walked down to the hotel, shooting anyone they saw along the way. Later, we got CCTV footage of them doing it.

Then they shot up the security guards in the carpark, before making their way into the lobby. There was also footage of a big guy with a machine gun walking down the side of the hotel and shooting an unarmed man sitting in a room. The rest of the group went down to the lower floor, where the hotel workers were. As they were moving through, they laid IEDs consisting of grenades on trip wires for later on.

Eventually, they went up the stairwells and got onto the roof. They'd obviously already been there and done a recce, or had guys onsite calling them on. They definitely had a plan, and they knew where they were going and what they were doing. Once they got onto the roof, they started sending guys down to search for guests. The comms we were getting through one of our operators said they were going to pull people out of their rooms, take them to the roof and cut their heads off, before throwing them off the roof of the building. We had to move fast to prevent that from happening.

So, leaving the rest of the boys outside the inner cordon, Steve and I crawled closer and got into a position where we could get a better view of the hotel's ground floor. As we sat there, the gun battle continued in front of us. The terrorists were still shooting off the roof, and down on the ground the Afghan forces were firing all over the place. The whole front of the hotel was pockmarked with rounds – they weren't good shooters, and they didn't have night vision capability. At the same time, guests on the upper floors of the hotel were tying sheets to the railings and jumping out of their rooms to try to get away from the gunmen.

Steve and I ascertained that to get inside the hotel we would have to run about 40 metres across the carpark, during which time we'd be exposed to the shooters on the roof. That was the only way in. So we made a plan, then went back down and briefed the boys. 'We're going to run one by one from behind the inner cordon here to those sheltered concrete walkways,' I said. 'From there, we'll head inside.' Doing it one by one like this would make it harder for the guys on the roof to shoot us, and it worked.

Inside the lobby it was pitch black. Prior to our arrival, a hotel security guard had already downed one terrorist. The body was lying on the ground, and he was wearing a suicide vest, so I had to assume the rest of his cohort did too. I got our explosive ordnance disposal guys to clear that straight away. Then the CRU mentors inside told us what had happened: they'd gone into the lobby and started making their way up the stairs, and that's when they'd come into contact with a guy who started shooting at them. The CRU kept their heads, and called out to the shooter, asking him to identify himself. He was the security guard who had dropped the terrorist in the lobby, and he thought they were terrorists. 'If you go any further,' he said, 'I'll shoot you.'

'We're police,' they replied. 'Come down.'

So he did, and they saw that he'd been so scared he'd pissed himself. They triaged him out, did a quick clearance around the area to make sure they were secure, and that was when we arrived.

Together, we decided that we'd head down the corridor and try to find the fire stairs, as they're usually the easiest way to get to the roof, at the same time clearing the hotel floor by floor, systematically, so there were no surprises. The CRU guys hadn't done anything like this before – they'd only done single- or double-storey compounds in rural areas, and they certainly hadn't done any complex operations in five-storey hotels at night. Plus they'd only just got their NVGs and were still training with them. It was out of their league at that particular time. So I said, 'Let's put our assault group at the front, and the CRU guys can follow us. We're going to have to lead the way this time.' It was what we had to do, and we wanted to do it. If we didn't, we were going to get people killed.

Everyone was good with that, so with Steve still in position as lead assaulter we started clearing down a corridor and moved into the internet room. We found the body of a guest leaning up against the wall with a half-written email open on the computer in front of him. We kept clearing down the corridor, then turned left, and made our way into the hotel kitchen. There, we found a door that, by chance, led to the fire stairs, and we pushed on up.

We started clearing the first floor with the CRU, then Steve came up on the radio. 'This is going to take too long,' he said. He was right. We were hearing a lot of noise coming from up top, so we decided to go straight up there, deal with the threat, then come back down to clear the floors and start releasing the guests, many of whom were still holed up in their rooms.

We headed back to the stairwell, and made our way further up, with the Taskforce Assault Group leading, followed by the CRU squadrons. The stairwell was open and had a U-shaped stair configuration, so there were plenty of angles, and we could see up to the top and down to the bottom. Usually, we'd have climbed it silently to maintain the element of surprise, but as the CRU guys had never done it before, the gunmen heard us coming.

On the fourth floor, Steve walked around the corner to start climbing the next lot of stairs when he suddenly found himself a couple of metres from one of the insurgents, holding an AK-47. They both started firing at the same time, but Steve managed to shoot him first. This young terrorist fell against the wall, but was so full of adrenaline he managed to get back up and run all the way up the stairs to the roof. After he disappeared from sight, we heard the sound of an explosion. Later, we saw footage taken by the ISR platform that showed the big man with a machine gun coming over to talk to him, then walking away and around the exit room at the top of the northern stairwell, before moving towards the other end of the roof. At this point, the big fella put himself in the line of fire and at exactly the same time the young guy detonated his vest. They were both killed, which made our job easier.

There was another guy at the top of the stairwell, and he started shooting down at us. I heard Steve yell, 'Grenade!' The grenade flew down and hit the stairs, then started bouncing down towards Steve, who ran through a door and into the hotel corridor. Almost as if it was attached to him by a string, the grenade followed him, then blew up behind him and dropped him on his arse. Our Peltor headsets cut out the noise – the microphone shuts off anything loud and in close proximity – but we saw it all.

Meanwhile, the gun battle in the stairwell continued and grenades kept getting dropped on us by the insurgent at the top. There were now two guys behind me, and I said to them, 'Spot that guy up there and kill him.' They got to work on that while I took the chance to check on Steve. But when I yelled out to him, he didn't reply. To get to him, we'd have had to cross the open area of the stairwell, exposing ourselves, while still taking grenades and gunfire … But then I saw him walk back out of the corridor and into the doorway leading into the stairwell. He'd got shrapnel up his back, and in his legs and arms, and he was semi-concussed, but when I asked if he was all right he just said, 'Yeah, yeah. Yep.'

We laid down some heavy covering fire, killing the insurgent at the top, which gave Steve the space to run back to where we were. After that, I decided that we'd go back down one floor, then move to the other stairwell to see if we could make another attempt at entry onto the roof – moving on a heavily armed insurgent at the top of a stairwell isn't a great idea, and could have cost us some lives.

It was at this point that I realised that, even with everything that was going on, I was as calm as anything. I could see everything that was going on around me in my mind's eye – what was happening on the roof, and on the stairs, and who was down there, and what was happening all around. My brain was staying ahead of everything, and seeing what was going to happen. I'd never had that before. I was just calm and in a flow state. It made it easy for me to make decisions, rather than having to stop and take every element into account in the midst of the chaos. Looking back, I can see how all my experiences on previous operations and training exercises had culminated towards that one point.

Once inside the third floor, I discussed an adapted plan with the CRU squadron commander. By this time, there were CRU guys holding every floor, and that gave us the ability to start getting the guests out of their rooms and to safety. The mentors started releasing the guests down the protected fire-stair route to the secure area in the kitchen, but getting people out of their rooms was hard. The guys would knock on each door and shout, 'Open up!' but the guests weren't sure whether to trust them.

Meanwhile, I decided that a smaller group from our team would move quietly across and up the southern stairwell located on the other side of the building, while the group that stayed behind would make enough noise in the northern stairwell to keep the remaining terrorists on the roof focused in the opposite direction. So, I took a smaller SAS team and a couple of the CRU members, and we climbed to the top of the southern stairwell, silently this time, so we could maintain the element of surprise when we hit the roof.

But, when we finally got to the top, the door to the roof had a metal bar across it with a padlock on it, preventing a soft entry.

'Let's put a charge on the door and blow it off its hinges,' I said.

One of the guys quietly put the charge on the door, and we all went back down a flight of stairs to take cover from the blast. We could still hear shooting up on the roof, and only had vague information on how many terrorists remained up there. So I called back down to the fourth floor on the radio: 'Hey, we're probably going to need a couple more CRU guys here if they're up to it.' Three agreed to come up. At least I knew they were legit, because they were keen to get in and help.

That was more than I could say for my interpreter. I needed him right beside me, so I could talk to the CRU – he'd come to us from a US special forces unit, and was always telling me how awesome he'd been, especially during operations, and how many engagements he had with enemy forces, but now he just kept running away! 'Man, stay on my hip!' I said to him. 'Do you wanna be paid? Because you won't be if you don't stay on my hip.' But he didn't stay with me. Can't blame him, really. It was a bit intense!

The walls were so thick where we were in the hotel that radio comms were intermittent, so I had to call back to our HQ group in Camp Warehouse on my cellphone. 'We're in final assault position,' I said, meaning we were ready to go.

'Roger that,' came the reply. 'Stand by.'

Our Taskforce HQ could see everything happening above us on the roof. We'd left two of our guys – the snipers – behind at Camp Warehouse, and they'd got on a Blackhawk. The helo sniper platform had been running circuits around the hotel, and while we'd been busy with our little gun battle in the stairwell they'd been engaging some of the terrorists on the roof and had killed a couple. There'd been a lot of incoming and outgoing fire going on between them and the insurgents on the roof, and at one point I'd glanced through the window in the stairwell half expecting to see a helicopter spinning past out of control like in the movie *Black Hawk Down*.

The whole time, our Taskforce HQ was coordinating things with the helo circling above to give us – the ground force – the best possible opportunity to succeed. And, as we stood there in the dark, waiting for a few quiet moments for them to give us the call to go, we took the chance to place fresh magazines on our weapons. I found myself thinking about those WWI soldiers who sat there in the trenches, ready to go over the top, not knowing what fate awaited them. It felt like we were doing much the same thing.

Then I got comms from HQ that we were good to go, and I shelved my thoughts of what the future held for me and my team. It was time to focus on what had to happen right now. Usually, I would have done a battle brief to tell the boys where to be and when, but this time I just said to them, 'At the end of the day, we don't know how many guys are up there, but whoever is up there, just drop them. I'll see you on the other side. Stand by ... Stand by ... GO!'

Then the door was blown off its hinges, and we threw grenades ahead of us to clear the space, then started making our way up to the roof. Once we were all up there, we got into an extended line, and moved south to north across the roof. In front of us was a bunch of satellite dishes mounted on half-metre-high concrete platforms. Past them was a large shed-looking building that housed the mechanism responsible for moving the elevators up and down. We started firing in any places that the terrorists might have been hiding. One was lying under a satellite dish, but was quickly engaged. Then I saw a leg sticking out from behind another of the satellite dishes, so I started firing at it, then came back around and shot it. But then I saw it was just a leg – it had clearly been blown across there when that young terrorist detonated his vest earlier. And that's when I realised there was all this human flesh all over the place.

As we were moving around the elevator shed, one of our soldiers to the left of it got into a gun battle with what seemed to be the last remaining terrorist. They were both shooting. The terrorist poked his head round to the right of the elevator and saw me and another guy coming round from that side, and he must have known he was fucked because he just stepped back and blew himself up. *Boom!* These guys thought they were tough, but when it came down to it they weren't even prepared to fight. They'd been through and killed a whole lot of innocent civilians, then got on top of the roof, and now that the playing field was suddenly evened out, they blew themselves up. They took the cowardly way out.

We pushed on, opened the door to the elevator shed and cleared it with grenades, and kept moving until we'd reached the northern edge of the roof. Once there, we made sure the guy who had been engaging us from the top of the stairwell earlier was dead. Then we called down the northern stairwell to let our team know we had taken control of the top of the building. We left the terrorists' bodies in place, because we knew there'd have to be a criminal investigation into what had happened.

Then someone said, 'Hey, the fifth floor's on fire.'

I turned around, and that's when I noticed flames lapping up over the edge of the roof. A terrorist had set a function room below us on fire, but we'd been so focused on clearing the roof that we'd been completely oblivious to the fact until now. Not wanting to be cut off from the floors below, we hastily moved off the roof, and tried activating several fire alarms – but none worked! We started clearing people from the building and down into the kitchen area. There, they were searched and cleared to make sure there weren't more terrorists planted among them and handed over to the Afghan police. Once we'd cleared all the guests out, the CRU left.

The team and I still needed to get back up onto the roof to do a detailed Battle Damage Assessment (BDA), so we told the Afghan police to keep the guests where they were. It was important that they stay where they were until we told them to move – but what did the police do? They let the guests go in the early hours of the morning. They were all on their phones, trying to get hold of their embassies to help them get out of there. It was crazy, because the hotel was secure, so it was safe – or, at least, we thought it was.

*

By this time, it was daylight, and the Afghan firefighters had arrived – with AK-47s in tow – and put out the fire.

During our BDA, we tallied up the terrorist bodies and cleared them of weapons, equipment, documents and cellphones to then be handed over to the authorities. We also cleared the suicide vests that they hadn't had a chance to crack off. Then we went down to check out the fire damage, and while we were standing in the function room, a couple of European pilots came out of their rooms all done up in their uniforms, good to go in their white shirts and wheeling their bags. They just walked right through the room, where everything was melted and charred, said 'hi' as they passed us and wandered out as though the whole thing was no big deal.

I headed back up to the roof to relay to HQ what was going on – but while I was talking to them, firing started again on the western side of the hotel. The shots were coming from quite close by. That was when we discovered that one last terrorist remained. He'd hidden himself away in a room below us until the fire had been put out, and was now taking his chance at us.

And then someone *else* started firing at us, so we all took cover behind the southern stairwell entry point. *The terrorists must have planned to get us on the roof,* I thought, *so they could launch a counterattack from the hills ...* We sat there for a bit, then Steve and another guy crawled up to the edge and I joined them. Where the fuck was the shooting coming from?

We poked our head over the wall, and that's when we realised we were under fire from our own side on the inner cordon. When the last terrorist remaining had started firing on the western side of the hotel, the ANA and ANP guys on the inner cordon had begun shooting, too – but not where the firing was coming from. Instead, they were shooting up onto the roof, straight at us! We waved out, and they waved back, then stopped firing at us.

'OK, let's reorientate,' I said. 'There's one more terrorist. We're going to have to go and clear him. Put a fresh magazine on, and let's go down to the fifth floor.'

There was a balcony along the western side of the hotel that went out from where the function room was and along to where the elevators were. It was maybe 30 metres long. We poked our heads round and we could see a pile of rubbish that looked like pieces of an air-conditioning vent down there. Beyond that was some expended AK-47 brass outside the entry to the fifth floor. We knew that was where the terrorist had fired from, so that was the direction we needed to go in if we wanted to sort him out.

We got to where this pile of rubbish was, and I said, 'What do you reckon? Shall we throw a grenade into the doorway, or just a flash-bang?' We decided on a flash-bang grenade – they don't cause damage; they're just disorientating. In it went. *Bang! Bang! Bang! Bang! Bang!*

And the cordon started firing at us again.

Had it not been for the fact that the rails round the balcony had reinforced concrete slabs on the inside of them, we wouldn't have made it out alive. I thought, *I hope to god they're not going to shoot the fifty-cals, because if they are, we're gone.* Looking up at the wall, I could see chips coming off the concrete and could feel the vibration of the rounds hitting the other side of the concrete railings. This went on for a while, and we just sat there taking it. Then I saw an Afghan policeman poke his head round the corner and look at us, and I yelled at him, 'Fucking tell them to stop firing!'

That didn't work. I couldn't understand why this guy wasn't helping us out. I got on the radio and said, 'Someone needs to tell these guys to stop firing or we're going to fucking die here. Fucking do something about it!'

Up on the roof, the interpreters gave the guys down on the cordon the wave, and they finally stopped.

'Is everyone all right?' I asked.

'I've been shot,' said Steve.

'Where?'

'Through the head.'

And when he turned round, I could see that his head was pissing with blood and his ear was hanging off a bit. I checked the wound. 'It's gone in and out, man,' I said. 'I think it's gone through the side of your head.' I'd had enough. 'Ah, fuck this,' I said. 'I'm going to call it a day. Someone else can deal with this last guy.'

*

Down on the ground floor, Steve got sorted out and I said to the boss, 'Our nine lives are out today. We've been shot at a number of times, and twice from friendly forces on the cordon. It's a very chaotic environment, with no coordination between us and the ANSF now that the CRU have left. It's probably not going to end well from this point, so I'm going to arrange transport for Steve to get to hospital, then we'll come back.'

'Yeah, fair enough,' said the boss.

I did a handover to the Afghan commander at the bottom of the building, then picked up our vehicles from the outer cordon, and headed back through the city. But as we drove, I started to see CRU vehicles heading back towards the hotel. I got on my phone and called the ops room. 'Why are the CRU guys going back to the hotel?'

'They're going to go and sort out the last one left.'

'I thought the commandos were there to do it?'

'No, the commandos are on standby for further attacks in the city.'

So we turned right around and drove back to the hotel. When we got there, I said to the CRU, 'Right, you're going to break into five groups. Group one, do the first floor. Two, the second floor. Three, the third floor and so on. Just be methodical. Go through all those rooms again and make sure no one's in there, and we'll sit down here at the bottom if you need us. I'll keep comms with you, but this is your ball game. Do it, come back, report to me, tell me it's done, then we're out of here.'

The guys who were on the fifth floor went round the balcony the way we'd gone. When they crossed over the vents, they triggered an IED – the terrorists had hidden a grenade in there and it blew. One of the guys came running back down with a big chunk out of his arm. We ran up to the fifth floor, and found parts of the IED still there, so we got our EOD guys to drag it clear. And, just like that, we were back in it again, trying to sort out the last terrorist.

*

'He's in Room 524,' the hotel manager told me.

'How do you know that?' I asked.

'Someone saw him go in there, and he's come in and out a few times.'

'Are you a hundred per cent it's five-two-four?'

'Yes. I'm sure.'

We got the CRU up behind us, and walked into the corridor. They cleared the rooms while we provided cover down the corridor. Unfortunately, we had only a handful of entry charges with us, which were big enough to gain entry into compounds, but not right for blowing hotel-room doors. For 20 rooms, we would have needed 20 lock charges, which were small enough to do the job while doing as little damage to the room – and its occupants – as possible. We also had only limited shotgun solid shot for hinge attacks, and these ran out quickly. This meant we had to go for manual entry techniques – namely, a Halligan bar and our feet.

We started making entry into each of the rooms and they were all empty, and by the time we got close to 524 the CRU had worn themselves out. So one of our guys took over. He gave the door a kick, and it started opening. Seconds later, there was a massive explosion and everyone disappeared in a thick cloud of dust. Everything slowed right down for me at that point. I felt like I was watching a slow-motion video of the CRU making their way through the smoke. No one could believe what had just happened. I was just pulling them out of the way as they were coming past me. *What the fuck was that?* I was thinking. *Was it an IED attached to the door, or was it a suicide vest?*

Then I heard someone say, 'Man down,' and everything sped back up again. The smoke started clearing, and I could see the guy who'd kicked the door was on his arse, slumped up against the wall. He was a big guy – about 100 kilos without his body armour on. I grabbed him and pulled him into the next room. 'Are you all right, man?' He didn't say anything. I turned to the others. 'I'm taking him out. See if you can get any other casualties and pull them back.'

I made my way back to the elevator. There was a chair there, so I sat him down. 'Stay with us, bro,' I kept saying. 'Stay with us!'

The terrorist had just walked straight up to the door, waited for it to open, then gone *bang!* Our guy had taken the full blast. If it had been anyone else, they would have been dead, but he was such a big bloke that he'd taken it like a champion. He had taken some ball bearings and had cuts to his face, arms and legs. I could see he was going into shock, so I just yelled in his ear, 'Stay awake! You've got to stay awake, man.' That appeared to bring him back around a bit.

I started patching him up, but soon realised that, as the ground commander, I was needed elsewhere, so I got one of the boys to get in there and do it.

We pulled everyone out and that was it. That was *definitely* it.

Now I had two guys going to hospital. We were already a small group, and losing a third person would have had a real impact on our ability to operate effectively. I was also mindful of the fact we had another operation coming up in a few days' time. So I said to the boss, 'We're done. The ANSF can sort the rest of this shit out.'

We got to the bottom of the building, handed off to the ANSF, dropped our guy at the hospital, then headed back to Camp Warehouse for a quick debrief.

*

By the time I got back to the hospital, Steve had been discharged – with his ear sewn back on – and our guy who'd kicked the door was on his way to Germany. It turned out he'd taken a ball bearing to his shoulder that then ricocheted into his chest.

I saw him before he left, and we had a bit of a laugh. 'Those beers are going to be good where you're going!' I said. He was a deep thinker with a heart of gold, so it was good to know that he was going to be OK.

All up, from the start of the operation to picking Steve up from the hospital, it was probably ten hours. It felt like a lot longer though. One account said there were 17 people killed by the terrorists that night. It could be more, it could be less – but it would have been a hell of a lot more if we hadn't got the comms that they were going to start cutting people's heads off with knives and throwing them off the roof. You have to be a psychopath to do that stuff. A normal human being doesn't do that, regardless of what they've been through.

*

Within hours of the operation ending, I found myself – once again – on the front page of newspapers back home. A photograph of me, Steve and the rest of the team leaving the scene along with a couple of the other guys had been taken by an Agence France Presse photographer.

Steve wasn't wearing his helmet because of his injury, so he was easily identifiable. And the fact that he was bleeding from his head added to the drama of the image. It ended up being distributed worldwide, and was reproduced in the *Los Angeles Times*, the *New York Times* and the *Guardian* in London. Of those three, only the *Guardian* blurred our faces.

We got a bit of a rap over the knuckles from the regimental sergeant major for being caught on camera. I explained that we knew the outer cordon was 400 metres away, so we hadn't expected any photographers to have been allowed inside it. We'd simply rounded a corner and the photographer had been right there, and it was too late. But we'd learnt our lesson.

*

Another media source provided us with an interesting background to what had happened that night. The Taliban quickly claimed responsibility for the attack, and it was soon confirmed that the affiliated Pakistan-based Haqqani network had been behind the operation. It's thought that the attack was timed to coincide with a meeting of senior diplomats as part of the Afghanistan–Pakistan Joint Commission for Peace that was to take place in Kabul the following day.

When the Afghan intelligence service released footage that had been taken by a NATO drone aircraft that had hovered over the hotel, it was translated and screened on *Al Jazeera*. The footage showed two of the Taliban gunmen on the roof on the phone to their commanders in Pakistan. Their calls were recorded.

One of the conversations happened while we were still making our way up to the roof. A terrorist called Rohullah was talking to one of his handlers, Qari Younis, who was back in Pakistan. When Rohullah asked Younis what he should do about the guests hiding in their rooms, the reply was, 'Talk to each other. Those who have been given orders should go downstairs and fight. Some should stay on the upper floors, and don't waste your bullets. Use grenades and talk with each other. If you're in agreement, go and break down one or two doors. Or, if possible, throw a grenade into the room, then pull back. Or shoot out the door locks with a Kalashnikov. Whatever you do, make sure these guys don't get away, OK?'

The second conversation that was released took place between an attacker called Omar and a man identified as Badruddin Haqqani, who was on the US list of designated global terrorists. When Omar told Haqqani that he was being blinded by smoke from the fire, Haqqani suggested he change locations. Omar told him that wasn't possible, then confirmed that he had plenty of ammunition. 'God willing, I'm very relaxed, lying on this mattress waiting for them,' he said, and in response, Badruddin Haqqani could be heard laughing, then saying, 'God will give you victory.'

When I heard that I thought, *Well, he wanted to die – and we gave him that wish.* Omar was the last terrorist we'd found, and just one of nine terrorists who died that night. (As for Badruddin Haqqani, he was killed in a US drone strike in Pakistan on 24 August 2012.) The Intercontinental, the Western hotel up on the hill, was such a big-spec attack for them. They did it right when everyone was having dinner and while there was a wedding going on out the back.

The bastards in there who got killed to become 'martyrs' were given energy drinks, new shoes, new clothes and the chance to shed the strict rules they lived under for a while before they came over the border to blow themselves up. What they did just served to legitimise the existence of these big terrorist organisations. The real extremists were the ones at the highest end who sat outside the theatre of war and were funding it, making all the decisions and doing the strategic planning. Those big players were only interested in seeing the little guys do the job they were being paid for. The cannon fodder at the bottom aren't the real extremists – they're just the ones who bring the world's attention in and scare everyone, then get celebrated as some sad sort of war heroes.

*

A couple of weeks after the attack, the regimental sergeant major and the colonel commandant came over to visit us.

They talked to the embassy staff and said they wanted to visit the Intercontinental. We took them up with a security party, and just walked them through the place.

It was the first time I'd been back there since the attack, and being there in the daytime meant I could see everything for what it was. The hotel was in a real state; there was so much damage … We followed the same track that we'd taken all the way up through the stairwell. The whole stairwell was shot to bits, and there were pockmarks all over the concrete walls.

For a moment, I stood where I'd been standing coordinating things, and I looked up. I had a direct line of sight to the top of the stairwell where the terrorist had been firing down at us. All he'd have had to have done was get a bead on me, and he'd have taken me out. I was in his direct line of vision, but for whatever reason I didn't get hit.

I wondered why he hadn't given me a crack. He must have been able to see something moving down there, but he just didn't get me. Sometimes, I think it was just the hand of god. Someone must have been looking over my shoulder, because at any point it could have happened. At any point, I could have been killed.

We carried on up to the roof, which was still covered in blood and human flesh. Walking around up there again felt odd. It was strange going back there in the light.

11

THE REAPER

AFTER THE INTERCONTINENTAL, ONE of the boys said to me, 'That's probably the biggest operation we've ever been on.'

I thought about it. 'You reckon?' I wasn't sure.

'Well, you tell me what's been bigger than that,' he said.

He had a point.

But I didn't have much more time to dwell on the magnitude of the experience, because we were too focused on getting prepared for the next job. We didn't have psychs in country, so the boys stuck close together and keeping the team busy was a good idea. We were all aware that there was still another month left of our deployment, so there was still work to do.

Less than a week later, we headed out into the countryside to locate another HVT. He was the head of a network, and had been responsible for many attacks on coalition forces and the public. He'd killed quite a few people. The US special forces had been trying to catch him for two years and hadn't managed it, so they gave him to us to have a crack at.

We looked at the terrain, the information we had and what had happened in the past when he'd got away. He was highly mobile, and once he was spooked he would run to a cave system in the hills. Those caves just consumed people, so he'd live to fight another day. It was clear that speed was going to be vital in catching him. Initially, we were going to put in a cut-off team to prevent him from going anywhere, but it was just too risky because the location was right up the back of a basin that was bordered by a high feature off the main road in a remote area with very little in the way of approach or safe withdrawal routes.

'I know what we'll do,' I said. 'We'll take two motorbikes and use them to cut off his escape route.'

The boys hadn't been on motorbikes for a while, so they were keen as. Steve's ear was still all stitched up from being shot, but he assured me the doctor had given him the all-clear to come too. I took his word for it. We did all the planning at Camp Warehouse, and conducted a few rehearsals with the CRU to get them used to the motorbikes. That night we stood on the helicopter landing zone in Camp Warehouse, waiting for the choppers to approach. The helicopters flew as a package consisting of CH-47s (Chinooks) supported by AH-64 Apache Gunships and Blackhawks. Once they landed, the lead CH-47 flashed his undercarriage light, indicating to me to approach the aircraft. I walked over to the load master, and he passed me the comms cable, which I plugged into. After talking to the captain to confirm aircraft load-outs and any plan changes, I walked back to the teams to give them the green light to board.

Once on the aircraft, we lifted off and headed out to the target area. Every time we did a helicopter approach I always conducted a final rehearsal in my head – something I learned as a skydiver on the way up to altitude. I'd go through the phases in detail: approach, assault, reorg, withdraw, then the actions-on. I'd also mentally prepare for specific scenarios, and always ended it with a Rorke's Drift scenario, in which you have limited resources and are over-run. Then I'd tune back in and start focusing on the comms we were getting from the AH-64s, which were about a minute up ahead and relaying what was happening at the target area. The most crucial part of the comms we were getting was whether the helicopter landing zone was clear of any enemy force or 'hot', which would mean we were walking into a shit fight. Thirty seconds out, the captain called 'clear' on comms, and the load master pulled a blue Cyalume out and waved it in the air to indicate to everyone on board the landing zone was clear.

On our final approach, the AH-64s fired infrared illum rockets to light up the landing zone for the CH-47s, as there was no moon. But the illum was quite bright, and lit up the whole area so much that I initially thought the target we were moving in on had put it up.

Above: Willie Apiata (right) and me leaving Pashtunistan Square in central Kabul following the January 2010 Taliban militant attacks that left about 20 dead.
Philip Poupin

Left: Preparing for a high-altitude oxygen-assisted jump at the United States Special Forces (USSF) Military Freefall Course, Yuma Proving Ground, Arizona, 2006.

Eight-way skydive with USSF Military Freefall Instructors over Yuma, Arizona.

Steve Askin examining weapons and equipment captured post-contact with Taliban forces. This was just after the engagement that earned Willie Apiata his VC.

In May 2008 I became the first person from my family to visit the grave site of my great-uncle Ashton Herrick who died at El Alamein, Egypt, during the Second World War.

Meeting with members of the Hazara community. The Hazara were generally friendly to coalition forces and visitors. The same could not be said of some other ethnic groups in Afghanistan.

Training members of the Crisis Response Unit (CRU) to be proficient at fast-roping out of helicopters. This was to enable them to conduct operations supported by the Afghan Air Force.

On troop outriding duty (I'm on the right). Our job was to stay a couple of kilometres ahead of the rest of the troop, route-finding and providing early warning of any threats ahead.

On mobility operations west or south of Kandahar. These patrols were designed to gain 'ground truth': terrain and lines of movement, tribal locations, enemy positions and possible locations for forward operating bases or airfields. We were away from Kandahar Airfield for anywhere between two and four weeks.

Monitoring a CRU training exercise on the southern edge of Kabul.

The CRU staging forward prior to carrying out a High Risk Arrest (HRA) in Kabul City.

Pre-operation vehicle brief, Kandahar. These briefs were to ensure that everyone knew exactly what each vehicle going on the operation was carrying.

Steve Askin on recon flight south of Kabul. Steve was awarded the New Zealand Gallantry Star following the Kabul Intercontinental Hotel siege in June 2011.

CRU covert surveillance team prior to heading out on an operation.

Troop resupply of food, water, ammunition and spares in the field via a US Army CH-47 Chinook heavy-lift helicopter.

Me, Steve Askin and the rest of the team leaving the scene of the Kabul Intercontinental Hotel siege. Steve is bleeding from a bullet wound to the side of his head.

Agence France-Presse / Pedro Ugarte

'Guys, keep an eye on the hills,' I said as we got out, but I wasn't too worried because we still had the AH-64s around if we got into trouble.

As the assault teams started making their way to the Alphas (target buildings), the two motorbikes set off up to the west, and as predicted, the HVT and his bodyguard also started moving west, using the ground to their advantage. We knew from intel reports that the HVT always carried an AK-47, and his bodyguard always carried a grenade and a pistol on his belt. Looking ahead, I saw an infrared beam come down from overhead ISR, lighting up the position of the HVT and his bodyguard as they ran. There was no getting away now, sunshine!

The motorbike team made their way down into a wadi to close the gap, but unfortunately one of them got stuck, and they were both in there trying to sort it out. Meanwhile, the HVT and his bodyguard were still running, so I got our JTAC, who was directing Close Air Support, to get the AH-64s to put corralling fire near them in a bid to put them to ground. That would give the motorbikes time to get sorted. This tactic worked, and the HVT and his bodyguard stopped and put blankets over themselves, thinking that they wouldn't be able to be seen.

Steve came over the radio and explained that the other bike was out of action. 'What do you want us to do?' he asked.

'You go out there and sort them out,' I told him. 'I'll put an AH-64 on your shoulder to support you.' Normally, we would go out in pairs in this sort of situation, but there was no way we were going to let these two get away.

Steve jumped on his motorbike and rode towards where the targets were, then dropped his bike and started walking up. We watched what he was doing via an ISR feed overhead. As he was getting near, the bodyguard got up and started walking towards him. Then he started reaching into his waist belt and going for his pistol. Steve gave him a few commands in Pashto to stop, then took him out as soon as he saw the weapon. Once the bodyguard had been dropped, the HVT took the blanket off and put the AK-47 on Steve, so Steve dropped him as well.

Then his voice came over the radio: 'I've got both of them.'

Once we had secured the area, a lawyer and I went to look at the bodies. Sure enough, the bodyguard had a grenade and pistol, and the HVT had his AK-47 but was also wearing a vest with magazines. The lawyer and I confirmed their identities and we cleared the bodies and left them out there. We then boarded the helicopters and flew back to Camp Warehouse for breakfast.

Steve was nicknamed the Lone Wolf after that.

*

Our post-operation observation showed that the local villagers just left both bodies out there for days. In Islam, a person should be buried as soon as possible after death, both as a sign of respect to the deceased and because the bodies do not get embalmed. So leaving the bodies out there like that showed how little respect the locals had for both men.

The HVT had held that province in a tight grip for a long time. We knew his death would stop that – but only for a short time due to the usual power vacuum sucking someone else in.

At least the locals got a bit of a reprieve, I guess.

*

On 17 July, just two and a half weeks after the Intercontinental, a man turned up at the compound of Jan Mohammad Khan, one of President Karzai's aides in the city. The guards searched the man, then asked what he wanted.

'Can I talk to Jan Mohammad Khan?' he asked. 'I'm from his province, and I'm on hard times. I'm just wondering if he can help me out.'

'Come back later,' the guards told him.

He did, along with another man, at about eight o'clock that night. And for some reason, the guards didn't search him again. They just let the pair into the house. Once inside, the men shot and killed Jan Mohammad Khan and another MP, Hasham Watanwal.

The CRU responded, and we followed them into town. We only learnt the full details of what had happened once we got on site, from our liaison officer on the ground.

The CRU started to make entry into the ground floor, but the attackers were up above, so they started firing. One of the CRU guys got shot through the neck and killed, and a couple of other CRU members were wounded. They managed to kill one of the gunmen, but there was still one left, and he managed to hold everyone back.

To access the compound, we had to go through a neighbouring property. We explained to the security guards who were on duty why we needed to go through the house and they let us in. The man who lived there was either English or American and was holding a pistol. But what was he going to do about us being there – say no?

Once we were out there, I realised that the only way to the roof was up a rickety bamboo ladder. I sent the CRU up one by one. It wasn't designed to hold kitted-out special forces members, so I spent the whole time looking up waiting for the ladder to snap. But, by some sort of miracle, we all made it to the top with the ladder intact – only to find that there was a gap of about a metre and a half, four floors up, between where we were and the roof of Jan Mohamed Khan's compound. On both sides were some dodgy-looking railings.

I was the ground commander, but because we were there to enable the Afghan forces, we gave them the opportunity to see if they could resolve the stand-off. They decided to send one person over the gap at a time. There was still a bit of shooting going on downstairs, so we covered the first guy as he ran and jumped over to Khan's building.

And, as he ran, it looked like someone with a weapon was running towards him. I was sitting there with my weapon down, so I said to one of the boys who had his weapon up, 'Get him!' He put a round through the person – and that's when we realised the top of Khan's house was covered in mirrored glass and we'd been shooting at the guy's reflection. Since we were wearing our NVGs, we hadn't been able to see it.

The CRU squadron moved across the gap and we followed them. The CRU then started moving into the building and clearing. We were 99.9 per cent certain there was no one in there except for the terrorist, because the family and staff had been accounted for.

While the CRU started clearing their way through the building, we found another rickety ladder, put it across the gap, discussed a casualty evacuation plan to the street below and waited for further casualties. The mentors went down with their CRU squadron, and we stayed upstairs waiting for them to bring the stand-off to a conclusion. We sat up there for a couple of hours while a battle unfolded downstairs. I poked my head in to check on things periodically but wanted to leave them to it.

Down the street, we had a medic and a liaison officer working with the other ANSF units involved, and one of our guys was also out the front of the building, ready to receive casualties.

The last terrorist had holed up in a room, and the CRU had him cornered, but he wasn't about to give up. They made multiple attempts to gain entry and got pushed back by a large volume of fire. On one attempt, some of the CRU went into the room, and he unloaded a volley of rounds. In those few seconds, one of them got clipped and landed on his back, and the others ran out of the room. The terrorist went up to the guy who was still on his back and said, 'I see all your friends have left you behind. They're a bunch of cowards. Now you're going to die.'

The terrorist put five rounds into him, but the CRU member had his body armour on with plates that could absorb multiple rounds. He took some in the chest, but away from the vital areas. After that, he just played dead. He was in there for a while, so he started bleeding out.

I heard the other CRU members trying to call out to him. 'What's going on?' I yelled down to them.

'We've lost one of our guys in there,' they replied.

'OK. Are you going to do something about it? What are you going to do? Are you going to make entry?'

'We don't want to go in there. It's quite difficult.'

Meanwhile, the terrorist was on the phone, talking to his handler and relaying what had happened. He then got up and walked back into the room to the vantage point he'd been shooting people from earlier. As soon as he did that, the injured CRU member got up and ran out too. He was covered in blood, but he managed to get downstairs and out of the building. Our medic patched him up and sent him off to hospital.

At that point, I knew we were at a stalemate. It was taking too much time, and there was pressure coming from the political level to resolve this by dawn, which at that time of the year was around 5am. As soon as the sun rose, people would be up and about, which would make the whole situation more unsafe. It wasn't a good look for the CRU to have it go on so long. So I poked my head down and said, 'Hey, can you guys handle this or not? Do you want to do it? Or do you want us to come down and show you how to do it?'

They replied that they wanted us to do it. So we pulled all of the CRU squadron off into a central room at the same time as placing our guys into covering positions. I talked the CRU squadron commander through the plan. We also agreed – since no one else knew what was happening inside the building – that any credit for the operation would go to the CRU, regardless of whether they ended the situation or not. Then I made sure that the outer cordon had been cleared. I didn't want them shooting at us like they had at the Intercontinental. Instead, we put in our own marksmen and replaced the two CRU members who were covering the door that led to the gunman's firing position and a window he could possibly escape through.

The gunman had now gone back into the room where he'd shot the CRU member, and there was another room inside the one where he was holed up – the main room was a sewing room, and there was a smaller bathroom inside it and a sunken bath. He was heavily armed, but I knew we had him boxed in, so we had time to plan what we'd do next.

'What do you reckon, lads?' I said.

I could feel the tension in the air. There was a high possibility that someone could get killed here, and as I looked at each of the guys around me a weird thing happened: I pictured their families standing behind them. The guys gave me some suggestions, but no strong solutions. The final say sat with me. And I knew any decision I made would affect not only the mission but also potentially these guys' loved ones, in a really significant way. *Fuck, I hope nothing happens here*, I thought. But again, I shelved those thoughts; we had a job to do.

The problem we faced was that the terrorist had a firing position inside a fatal funnel, meaning the opening of an entry point where most fatalities occur. But, in this case, he was within depth and we were faced with two rooms meaning *two* fatal funnels. We therefore had to innovate and do something that we had never trained for. First, we decided to figure out which room he was in by using the door entry as cover – something we could do because the walls were thick concrete in this building. Then, once we knew where he was, the second part of the plan was to put an entry charge in line with his position and blow it, hopefully killing or incapacitating him enough to advance at speed, and then shoot him. We weren't going to take the risk of getting him alive, as we didn't know whether or not he had a suicide vest on – but we did know it was highly likely.

'We're not going to run to our deaths on this one,' I said to the boys. 'If it takes all night, it takes all night. I don't care. I'm not going to get any push from anyone outside. Slow and methodical.'

There was a murmur of agreement. We got ready, covered his exits, then Steve and one other rounded the corner. They were greeted with a huge weight of automatic fire coming back at them through the door in depth. 'Yep, he's definitely over here,' said Steve when they came back. He pointed to the wall where he thought best to place the charge.

Since the walls were so thick, our internal entry charges weren't designed to do the job, so we had to use our external entry charges instead – a higher-weight charge that had the necessary power to punch through the wall. The charge was placed in about ten seconds, and everyone took cover in the rooms parallel to where this guy was. I was standing around the corner from where the charge was being set off, then *BOOM!* It was like someone had taken a baseball bat to the back of my legs. This was because the overpressure or shock wave from the charge had to navigate a confined solid space as it made its way out through the doors and windows. It was horrendous, but it wasn't the first time I'd experienced it. Later, I saw the footage from the ISR platform overhead, and when the charge went off, every single window and door on that floor got blown out.

After the charge blew we sat and listened. We could hear groaning and sounds like he was rolling around and wounded, so we thought it was a good chance to get in there and finish it. We made an attempt at getting into the room, but got another huge wave of fire. This guy was hard! That left us with a bit of a dilemma.

There were only two ways he could get out: through the rear window, or through the door he was shooting through. We discussed using another entry charge. 'Nah, don't waste your time,' I replied. 'Let's throw grenades in until he falls silent.'

Steve and I positioned ourselves on either exit. I threw a grenade in. *Boom!* We waited. He was still moving around, but now the room was on fire. So Steve threw another one in. *Boom!* We waited. He was still moving around ... but now the room *wasn't* on fire. The grenades were starting fires, then putting them out. We just kept grenading the room until we didn't hear anything. It turned out he was in the sunken bath – it was protecting him, and all the shrap was going across the top – and it took 14 grenades to kill him. By then, the whole area was absolutely trashed and making entry to check would have been difficult.

I thought it a good idea to get rid of my body armour, take my pistol, climb through the hole left by the explosive charge, then clamber over the rubble to make sure the insurgent was taken care of. But the boys talked me round.

I decided the ANP could take it from there. The CRU had already lost one, maybe two and had a few wounded in hospital. I wasn't prepared to risk our lives any further, just to make sure the terrorist was dead. Dawn was breaking, and we couldn't hear anything coming out of the room for a while, so we called the ANP forward to do the final clearance and clean-up.

*

The Taliban later claimed responsibility for that attack. It took place on the same day that responsibility for the security of Bamyan province was handed over to Afghan forces. This was the first province to regain control of its own security, which was a huge achievement for the New Zealand troops in the Provincial Reconstruction Team, and a real testament to the connection they had made with the local people.

One of our next jobs took us through the base at Bamyan. It was another night mission, and I was ground commander. The plan was to take the CRU, land at Bamyan, get something to eat, then fly into Baghlan. For the operation, we had the usual Helicopter Assault Force package. The goal was to conduct a high-risk arrest on three HVTs who had just carried out an attack on a local ANP checkpoint and killed ten policemen. Our intel told us they'd been skiting about how awesome it had been to kill the policemen, and given they were together we thought it was highly likely they would oppose our approach and entry.

The weather wasn't looking too sharp, but the mission was still a go. Sitting on the helicopter landing zone at Camp Warehouse, we could see thunder clouds building. I thought we'd be able to get around them, so we got into the helos and started our approach. We had to fly over a mountain range that went up to about 12,000 feet, then down the other side and into Bamyan.

As we flew into the storm, I could hear the comms on the radio. The pilots were getting increasingly worried. 'Yeah, I don't know about this ...' I heard one of them say. 'I'm not too sure if we're going to get over this mountain range.'

'I think we'd better call back to headquarters,' said the pilot. 'Can the ground commander see this in the back?'

'Yeah, I can see it,' I replied. I had NVGs on, and I could see the helicopters behind us being lit up by lightning flashes.

'I don't know about this, sir ...' the pilot said again.

He wasn't just uncomfortable about flying during the lightning storm. He was also worried about hitting the mountain because the visibility was so bad.

'Listen,' I said. 'No bullshit. If you think we're going to fly into the mountains, then we can abort the mission now.'

'Yeah, I just don't feel comfortable in this weather.'

Even with all the best military equipment – NVGs, radar,

everything – at his disposal, he was still agitated. Something was clearly wrong.

'Sweet. Mission abort,' I said.

So we carved our way to the left, and flew back to Kabul.

The next night, the same helo package went out on a mission with a bunch of Navy Seals on board, and one of their CH-47s got shot out of the sky by a rocket-propelled grenade. All 30 Seals and crew on board were killed.

Usually, I would have been saying 'Let's go!' and pushing it because I knew the targets were out there and might kill again, but something just hadn't felt right that night. I couldn't help but think that the reaper had been out there, ready to take either us or them. I knew I'd made the correct decision, even though I had to front the SNO to explain and justify my choice.

*

At the end of our deployment, we spent two weeks doing transition with the new crew. Half our team stayed, and another half came in. That way, there was always some experience there and it wasn't a completely fresh crew.

We took the new guys out on a couple of jobs, warmed them up, did the handovers and the meet-and-greets, then we ended up having a few beers. We weren't on standby anymore, and we'd handed over, so we got stuck in. We hadn't been drinking in three or four months, but we drank like it'd been yesterday.

Beer, whiskey, whatever ... I woke up at four o'clock in the morning outside the barracks. Someone had put a sheet over me.

That day, we had to get our gear packed and into the trunks, then weighed for our Air-Move Rep to put onto the planes. I was so hungover, but I managed to pack my trunks and take them over to the scales. The air-move guy was sorting someone else out, so I lay down on the concrete, closed my eyes and had a bit of a moe.

We were right outside the workshop area. One of the mechanics got into an armoured vehicle, started it up and started driving it out. I could hear it coming closer, so I opened my eyes. No shit, the bumper was inches away from me! Despite my hangover, I managed to roll out of the way quickly, otherwise he would have run me over. I would have been gone.

I still give him shit about the time he nearly killed me. But at the time, I thought, *Jamie, you absolute idiot!* Then I decided I was never drinking again – and it was the last time I got drunk in my life.

*

Having completed the handover, we got on the plane and flew out to Camp Bastion in Helmand province. We overnighted there, and when we got up on the morning of 19 August heard that there was a job going on in Kabul. The British Council building was under attack.

It was the same thing we'd dealt with at the Intercontinental. The terrorists had gone in, carried out the attack, and the media were giving them the attention they so wanted. The CRU had arrived, and we could see some of our guys on television. Then we saw one of the boys getting stretchered out to a helo on the ground. It was Duggy Grant. I'd known Duggy a long time, as he had been in 1st Battalion at the same time as me, and was on the cycle of training before mine. We also shared an interest in riding motorbikes, and had gone on rides together with the Patriots Motorcycle Club.

When we rang the ops room, they told us he hadn't survived.

He had a family back home – a wife and two kids who had no idea what had just happened. I knew his wife, Tina, as we'd been on our Senior Non Commissioned Officers course together, and I could only imagine the life-changing hurt that was about to fall on her and her kids.

Duggy was the first New Zealander to be killed in action in Afghanistan. That really affected all of us, and it was a solemn group that flew out of Afghanistan to Dubai later that day, then on to New Zealand a week later.

*

Going from Afghanistan to Dubai to New Zealand within a week was wild. We saw the pyschs, did a bit of shopping and suddenly I was standing at my front gate in Papakura again. I felt like I was in a dream. *Am I really here?* I couldn't help wondering. Three quarters of my being was still over there. It was such a weird feeling.

We met with the psychs again a day or two after we arrived in New Zealand so they could check what was going on for us. But back in those days, if you said, 'Nah, it's all good', then that was that. I didn't want to talk to the psych, so the only people I could talk to were the boys who'd been there with me. So I pretty much just came home, didn't talk much about what I'd experienced, then after about three weeks' leave got right back to work.

One of the first training sessions I did was at the parachute school, and we'd just finished doing some skydiving when I got a call from the OC. 'Have you heard?' he said.

'Heard what?'

'Leon Smith has been killed.'

Leon had been part of a team enabling the CRU during a high-risk arrest of an HVT in Wardak. He'd climbed a ladder to provide cover into the compound before the assault group made entry. Unfortunately, a man ran out and opened the door below where Leon was, produced a pistol and shot him through the head. The guy was then shot and injured by the CRU as they assaulted the compound.

Leon's close friend had helped attempt to stabilise him, but his injuries were catastrophic; he was taken to the helicopter landing zone to be transferred to higher medical aid. And, while that was happening, his mate had turned his attention to the man who'd shot him. He saved the guy's life. I have no doubt that this was an incredibly difficult thing to decide to do, but it's an example of the professional culture that exists within all ranks of the regiment, whether in training or on operations.

Leon had been on his second deployment, and he was the one who had dragged Duggy Grant out of the British Council building – an action for which he was later awarded the Charles Upham Award for Bravery. I wasn't close to Leon, so although I found the news about his death sad, I also took the matter-of-fact view that it came with the job. Probably to make it easier for me to absorb and not dwell on. I also had to let the rest of the boys I was training with know about Leon's death, so I gathered them together in a room to break the news. One of the boys who was close to him was visibly upset. I decided to take him back to Papakura.

Losing two guys in Afghanistan in little more than a month was pretty dire. I found it hard, because I kind of felt like I should have been there. Like maybe I could have done something to prevent their deaths. Of course that wasn't the case, but I felt partly responsible anyway. It was especially tough for the guys who had transitioned into the team with Duggy and Leon. To have two of your mates die was a heavy burden to carry.

12

LIFE CHANGES

I'VE SAID I DIDN'T want to talk to the psychs about what I'd experienced, and that's true. But there was *one* psych who worked for the regiment that I did take a bit of a shine to when I first met her – but it was for entirely different reasons.

Alia lived in Christchurch, and was part of the pool of psychologists who provided pysch support across all three services. She'd been picked for the regiment because she was highly competent, and as part of her role with the regiment she provided psych services during selection courses in Auckland. When we first met, pursuing a relationship had been off the cards. For one, we both had partners, and for another, she was an officer – a captain – while I was a non-commissioned officer. It just wasn't the done thing. But when I went down to Christchurch for work and she invited me around to her house for dinner, I thought maybe she was interested … Maybe I was in with a chance! But I was soon set straight when I discovered that's just the way she is. It's the Bulgarian way. Dinner was just dinner, and then it was, 'Here's your bed and I'll see you in the morning.'

When she was next in Auckland, she got in touch. I told her I wanted to reciprocate, and she'd have to come around to my place for dinner. And, after that, we started seeing each other. She was still working for the regiment, so that made things tricky, as did the fact I had already started doing pre-deployment training for my fourth trip to Afghanistan. I ended up telling her, 'I'll see you when I get back, and if things pick up from that point, so be it.' I didn't want the distraction while I was gone. I wanted to be able to focus on my work, and I thought having someone I cared about back home could affect how I did my job.

But the whole time I was away, we stayed in touch online … and our relationship just continued to grow. Alia is a very unique woman in my eyes – she's beautiful, intelligent, quirky, high energy and driven, among a lot of other things! I missed her, and she missed me. So, at the end of 2012, only a year after we began seeing each other, we got married. We celebrated our wedding with our families at a lodge just north of Kerikeri and off the beaten track a bit, with no cellphone coverage. We had dinner delivered by a local chef, and just ate and drank into the night, then stayed for the next two days as well.

And two months after that, we were on a plane to Israel. Alia already had worked lined up there with the UN, and she'd asked me to go with her. She thought it would be a good opportunity for me to decompress after a full-on few years. So I took a year's sabbatical, and enrolled to do a bachelor's degree in training and development by distance learning through the University of Armidale in Australia.

Taking time away was a good thing, and landed at the right moment. Over the years, I'd put all my energy into the regiment and its mission, but I was starting to have intermittent memory loss and was constantly fatigued, no matter how much I slept. I felt like I was pulling myself around by the scruff of the neck! Looking back, I can see I was definitely burned out, but I wasn't explicitly aware of it – so that meant I went to Israel and just maintained the same pace. Different place, different tasks, same approach.

*

Alia operated as part of Operation Scoria, which is the United Nations' longest-lasting peacekeeping mission. The United Nations Truce Supervision Organization (UNTSO) has been in place to monitor Arab–Israeli peace since 1948, and New Zealand has supplied observers since 1954, with up to eight military personnel deployed in Lebanon, Syria and Israel at a time. It was an interesting time for her to be going to do that work, as the Syrian Civil War had kicked off in 2011.

We stayed in Jerusalem while Alia was doing her pre-deployment training, and still waiting on information about her placement. The options were Tyre in Lebanon, Damascus in Syria, or Tiberias in Israel. We ended up in Tiberias, which overlooks the Sea of Galilee, opposite the Golan Heights. And, while Alia was out doing her work, I studied. It was new territory for me, and my first attempt at writing an essay was a bit of a laugh. Alia had said she'd coach me through it, so I sent her the first one, and when she got me on the phone said, 'Did you write this?'

'Yeah.'

'Are you sure?'

'Yeah.'

'How did you do it?'

'I just read through the research articles, then took chunks of them and copy-and-pasted them into the essay, with a bit of me talking in between.'

'You know you can't do that, right? You've got to read the research, present and argue a concept, then provide an example with references. Then keep doing that all the way through.'

I learnt the hard way, but by the end I'd cracked the code for essay-writing and was managing to bang out one a week.

In the evenings, I trained in Brazilian jiu-jitsu (BJJ) and mixed martial arts (MMA) at a really good gym in Tiberias. The gym owner was a guy by the name of Roy Peretz, who taught the Royce Gracie BJJ system – a self-defence style of jiu-jitsu that not many BJJ gyms do (most teach the sport style, and this is totally different). I was going there four or five times a week and training with a bunch of cool Israeli guys. They were a very tough and staunch bunch, and they looked after me while Alia was away – which was most of the time. At the end of the year, Royce Gracie came over for grading. I was successful at the grading and received my blue belt from him.

One morning, while Alia was out at an observation post in Syria close to the Israeli border, I got a knock on the door while I was studying. It was the operations officer. 'Hey, Jamie,' he said. 'Can I come in?'

What's this all about? I wondered. I was a bit worried.

'I just wanted to let you know that Alia and her crew were taken hostage last night ...'

Fuck. My heart started to race.

'... but they've just been released, and they're in a camp up in the Golan Heights, going through a debrief process and full medical check.'

It was a scary situation. I knew Alia was alive, but that was all. My brain ran through a whole pile of scenarios about what might have happened. Had she been beaten up or tortured? Or worse?

When she got back, she seemed OK. She said that their compound had been surrounded by about 30-odd armed militia, and one of her team members had sent the SOS call to UN HQ. They then walked through a minefield in a no-mans-land area between the Israeli and Syrian border, before being taken to an old house on the Syrian side. There, they were questioned. Alia started building a rapport with the militia group's leader, and negotiating an audience with the UN chief. They were then released, and crossed over onto the Israeli side the next morning. And that was about all she said. She didn't really want to talk too much about what had happened.

It gave me a bit of a scare, and she ended up having a couple of other close calls while on the line. But Alia was keen to continue the work she'd gone to do, so that's what she did.

*

We took a bit of time off during our trip there, and decided to do some travel. We went to Bulgaria, Alia's birthplace, and to Jordan, Turkey (for ANZAC Day in Gallipoli) and Thailand. Then after about seven months in Tiberias, and a few months after the incident in Syria, Alia took up a HQ position in Jerusalem, and we stayed there for the next five months. In Tiberias, it had been really hot, but winter in Jerusalem was cold and it snowed, which made for a decent Christmas Day. We saw a lot of the country while we were there, too, including Tel Aviv, the Golan Heights, Masada and Elat. It's an amazing place.

During our time in Jerusalem, we lived in East Jerusalem, a Palestinian area just outside the walls of the West Bank. And, even though we weren't actually *in* the West Bank, there was still a lot that we couldn't get because of where we were. For example, I wanted to get cable TV – but because we were in a Palestinian area, no one would come install it. I told one guy that I'd meet him at the bottom and walk him in, and that no one was going to do anything, but he still refused.

The same thing happened when I was coming back in a taxi from watching a Brazilian jiu-jitsu fight in Tel Aviv one evening. When the driver asked where I lived, I just told him 'in Jerusalem'. But when we got nearer to my place, he asked, 'Where *exactly* do you live?' I told him, and straight away he said, 'Oh no! I can't go in there.'

'Yeah, you can,' I said. 'Chill out, mate.'

He would have been completely safe, but he'd probably spent his whole life hearing and seeing the worst of what happened there, and had become indoctrinated.

Our landlord, Mohammed, was a really good guy. He was a prominent figure in the community, so our relationship with him greased the wheels for us. We had a pretty cool little apartment there, and the whole community was really accommodating. When we'd go into the local restaurant, we'd be the only foreigners there, and when we told people where we were living, they'd respond, 'Oh, yes, you're Mohammed's people. The New Zealanders.'

One day, we went in to get takeaways, and they gave us our order on a massive white platter covered with tin foil. I was a bit confused. 'What do you want me to do with the plate?' I asked.

'Just bring it back next time you come,' said the guy. 'It's all good.'

I loved having that sense of community. They knew who we were, and they looked after us.

*

That year away gave me some space to really think about what I wanted to do with my life. Before I left Israel, I was pretty adamant that I wasn't far off stepping down from the regiment. During my break away, I'd started to see some opportunities I'd never seen before. I realised there were other things I wanted to do. And Alia also had things that she wanted to achieve away from the military.

However, before taking my sabbatical, I'd signed a Return of Service Agreement that required me to serve a compulsory two-year period upon my return. It was standard organisational practice – the New Zealand Defence Force had taken care of my degree, and this ensured they got value back from me after those studies. So, when I got back to New Zealand in 2013, I ended up straight back in the thick of it and I was soon consumed by the job again.

I'd been shoulder-tapped to become an officer a couple of times during my career. I often questioned why, and my peers did too! Once was when I was a corporal, but they'd wanted me to go to officer cadet school in Waiouru for a year so I passed on that offer. The second time, I was asked by my OC, but I said no because we were quite staunch in the regiment about ORs (Other Ranks) staying the course through the OR stream. There was a bit of friendly banter, but the boys would never cross from one side to the other – unless they topped out and wanted to commission as a Warrant Officer Class 1 in the regiment. This was standard. Otherwise, the officers did their thing, and we did ours. We were two separate rank groups, and that was it. The last time someone had crossed over was back in 1995.

But when I got back from Israel I decided I actually *would* like to be an officer. I just didn't want to have to go through the prescribed process of NZSAS officer selection, which was discussed briefly. The fact I'd completed the unit capability command courses in both black and green roles, along with everything that had happened on my last tour – where, as a sergeant, I'd been given full control of a small troop and coordinated Task Forces numbering anywhere between 60 to 140 personnel out on jobs – all worked in my favour. However, I still had to go through an Officer Selection Board, as does anyone commissioning from the ranks. This took place over five days in Wellington, and involved additional psychometric testing, writing essays, being interviewed and presenting plans for unorthodox problems both individually and as a collective group. Six of us presented for selection and four passed, including myself.

When I returned from the Officer Selection Board, I had a discussion with the RSM about my future as an OR. The RSM wanted me to carry on as an OR and attend the next Warrant Officers Course in a few months, with a view to becoming a Squadron SSM a few years later. I'd always had an ambition to become the RSM of the regiment – as did my peers – but when I did the math I figured that was ten years away, or more. I would be about 50 by that point, if the current line of ORs ahead of me stayed the course.

So I went to see the CO about my future as an officer. Initially, I thought I wouldn't be considered to command a troop, but the CO set me straight.

'Just prepare to be treated the same as any other troop commander,' he said, 'and expect to complete all the officer courses.'

That's when I decided to commit to being an officer. I wanted to stretch and develop myself in both familiar and unfamiliar territory, and see how I fared in the officer stream. I stayed as a staff sergeant for the rest of the year, and was then commissioned from the ranks and promoted to acting captain the following year and took over as troop commander for air/mobility troop.

For a while, some of the senior members were a little bit funny with me because there was a trajectory I hadn't followed. They were probably quite shocked that I'd become an officer, because I had been a real staunch OR, and hadn't hesitated to point the finger at them from time to time when I thought they needed it. Me going across as an officer – no one would ever have picked that!

*

Towards the end of 2014, the CO called me into his office to give me a letter. 'Read this,' he said.

I did, then looked up at him. 'Are you sure?' I said.

'Yes,' he replied. 'I'm going to announce it to the regiment tomorrow.'

After we'd got back from Afghanistan, I'd put everyone who was involved with the Intercontinental up for a medal – everyone except myself, that is, as that would have been a bit wrong. For me as the ground commander on that tour, I was lucky enough to have a well-gelled team and they *all* performed exceptionally well that night.

From that initial application, all the information then went through a whole lot of different levels of scrutiny. From the regiment, it goes through the upper levels of the Defence Force, then to the government, then – in the rare case of a

Victoria Cross – to England for royal assent. This all takes a few years to process.

The next day, in front of the whole regiment, the CO announced that five regiment members were awarded the New Zealand Gallantry Medal, and two were getting awarded the New Zealand Gallantry Decoration for their actions at the Intercontinental and the British Council Office.

What's more, Steve was being awarded the New Zealand Gallantry Star, which is the country's second-highest military honour for bravery, after the Victoria Cross.

And so was I.

*

The awards were handed out at a private ceremony at Government House in Wellington. Governor General Sir Jerry Mateparae was there, and as soon as he saw me he smiled. After all, we'd got to know each other quite well on our trip around the Middle East.

When announcing the awards, the then-Minister of Defence, Gerry Brownlee, said, 'Our NZSAS personnel operate in dangerous and volatile situations, and all of these men have demonstrated extreme courage in the face of a determined enemy.'

That's exactly why I felt that everyone who was on the Intercontinental operation should have received awards, as they all put themselves at the same level of risk.

Steve's citation read:

Serviceman S displayed outstanding gallantry on several occasions in Afghanistan in 2011. Corporal Askin repeatedly faced heavy fire from determined enemies and sustained several wounds in the line of duty, while contributing to the resolution of several incidents, the protection of civilian life and undermining enemy operations. Corporal Askin's performance was of the highest order and in keeping with the finest traditions of New Zealand's military record.

Mine said:

Serviceman J attended an incident in Kabul, Afghanistan in 2011. Serviceman J demonstrated outstanding gallantry and leadership under heavy fire from a determined enemy, contributing to the resolution of the incident and the protection of comrades and civilian life. Serviceman J's performance was of the highest order and in keeping with the finest traditions of New Zealand's military record.

It was a pretty amazing experience to be at Government House with so many regiment members and our families, but it still felt a bit awkward. I don't think I know one person in the regiment who likes being talked about or recognised. The nature of our work means we all find it pretty uncomfortable, so the humility part of 'humour and humility' really comes to the fore at times like that.

If I'm honest, I was expecting Steve to get the VC for his actions that day. He was relentless. He went face to face, stood his ground and shot a terrorist. Then he got blown up by a grenade and got shrapnel in the back, but when he was asked if he wanted to leave, he said no. He wanted to stay with it. Semi-concussed, he led the group up the northern and southern stairwells, did his job and got shot through the side of the head, but *still* wanted to stay on until I told him he'd had enough and had to go. That's the kind of guy you want by your side.

13

SNAPPED AGAIN

IN SEPTEMBER 2015, I FLEW into Iraq on a confidential reconnaissance, planning and preparation operation. Our destination was Taji, which was the base for about 100 New Zealanders who were working alongside Australian troops to train Iraqi security forces. This time, though, I wasn't there to help with training. Instead, my job was to prepare for a visit by the New Zealand Prime Minister, John Key.

A small team of us went in to check the areas we would be visiting, and to create our security, movement and accommodation plans. Camp Taji was big, and it had a lot of locals working there. This meant that there was a risk that word could get out that we'd been there, so we needed to get in and out without raising suspicion. Knowledge of the PM's visit by any threat groups needed to occur *after* he had left the country. We didn't want people to know that he would be arriving soon, as that would give them time to plan for a possible attack either inside or from outside the wire, which occurred fairly regularly.

Usually, we walked around with long hair, looking pretty rough, in order to not raise suspicions when we were on the ground – but turning up like that would have definitely raised suspicions in a conventional camp. So, instead, we rolled in with fresh army-regulation haircuts and wearing the same emblems as the other Kiwi soldiers, looking like we'd just arrived in the country. There were a few soldiers who recognised us but knew not to say anything.

We did all our rehearsals, met everyone, made sure we were squared away, and had a shisha at a café on a boardwalk where people were drinking tea and getting haircuts. Then, with everything checked at Taji, we flew into Baghdad to conduct further planning and preparation alongside the NZ ambassador and private NZ military contractors who had been in country for over a decade. The city had a well-protected green zone and the security there was pretty solid. The only people driving the streets in the green zone were those who had been searched and cleared through checkpoints, however we always stayed on guard. There were a lot of guns and tanks on the streets, most of which belonged to the Iraqi forces, but there was some American military presence as well.

*

We met the prime minister and his entourage in Dubai. There were more people with him than I'd dealt with on the trips with Phil Goff and Murray McCully. Before we headed into Iraq, I held a briefing for everyone who was going. As well as the prime minister, there was the Chief of the Defence Force, the Warrant Officer of the Defence Force and the commander of the local camp. Then there were just rows of people – every Tom, Dick and Harry seemed to be in the room. We knew how many people we'd have on the aircraft, but there were three times as many people at the briefing.

'Is everyone coming tomorrow?' I said.

They just looked around at each other.

I started to wonder if we'd been given the wrong numbers. 'I've only got 15 people on my list who should be here today,' I said. 'So if you are not flying into Iraq tomorrow I don't need you to be in on this briefing. You can go.'

They kept looking around. They were all high-ranking officials, so none of them left.

I thought, *All right then, I'll play the game*. I knew no one was going to budge. They just wanted to be in on the brief. 'OK, well, we must all be going then,' I said. 'I'm going to have to increase our manifest.'

Then I went through the usuals – introducing myself and the team, then giving a detailed brief of where we would be going and what we would be doing. At the end, I went through what would happen if we came under attack. Then I said, 'If we do come under attack, you just need to know that the person we love the most in the group – the person who is priority number one for us – is the prime minister, and you will see that in our actions.'

The PM laughed, and said, 'Oh, yeah, thanks!'

I continued, 'So, what you'll see is that we'll be making sure he is well protected and, if need be, we'll extract him and get him out of harm's way. Just follow on! Priority two is the CDF. It's not that we don't love the CDF ... It's just that we don't love him as much as the prime minister.'

That broke the ice a bit.

I talked to them about attacks that had occurred from the north and coming into Taji. It was all fairly serious, but we still needed to give them confidence that we knew what we were doing. 'You're here to visit the place, so just do what you'd normally do on one of these visits,' I said. 'Don't worry about anything. We're here to do what we do. If anything kicks off, you've got to understand that the boys will be straight into it. That's what we're trained for, and that's what we're here for. Let us do our piece, and you guys do yours.'

After that, I sat with the PM in a room one on one and went through everything else we needed to cover, then asked if he had any questions about what was going to happen. With him, what you saw was what you got. He liked a laugh and to joke around a bit. He even took the piss out of me a couple of times. When I was in my suit, he said, 'Oh, Jamie, you don't really look like an SAS soldier. You look like a junior MP!'

He was really easy to talk to, and he was good at building relationships with people. He looked you in the eye the whole time he was talking to you, and always let you know he was listening. It was another instance of seeing just how hard these guys work.

*

When we were due to fly out to Baghdad, I did a head count and realised we were missing a journalist. 'Patrick Gower's supposed to be here,' I said. 'Where is he?'

The rest of the media contingent looked around at each other and had a bit of a laugh. One of the reporters said, 'Did you not hear?'

He'd left his passport in the hotel and gone back to get it.

'When did he leave?'

'Not long ago ...'

'Mate, he's not going to make the flight,' I said. 'It's going to take him an hour and a half to get there and back again.'

The gathered reporters laughed uncomfortably.

One of the other journos said, 'Yeah, he had to ring his boss and let them know.'

I knew he'd be in the shit, but there was nothing we could do about it. We were on a tight schedule to get the prime minister to Baghdad and on to Taji that day – so there was no way we could wait for him.

We flew up there in a New Zealand Air Force C-130 Hercules, but a massive dust storm blew through, making it too dangerous to try to land. So, instead, we headed back to Dubai, which was about a three-hour flight. When we got there, we found the secure airfield was under heavy fog, and after a couple of attempts to land, had to divert to Dubai International Airport. Since we were at a public airport, we had to leave all of our weapons, equipment and radios on the aircraft and get off with nothing. It felt really weird. By that time, it was three in the morning. The flight crew then had to have a lengthy stand-down period to rest before they could fly again, so that plane and everything in it was out of action for a while.

We handed the prime minister off to the police security team that we had in Dubai, and he went back to his hotel. As for us, we went back to our base camp and rolled through the gates, had breakfast, then spent the entire day zeroing in new weapons, configuring vests and setting radios. In terms of worst-case scenarios, losing all your gear before going into Iraq was pretty much it.

The only person who was happy about what had happened was Patrick Gower. It meant he was able to rejoin the trip, which – I guess – got him out of trouble with his boss. He was ready and waiting for us at the airfield later that day.

'You're lucky, man,' I said when I saw him. 'You're so lucky we turned round. It was an act of god, I reckon.' Then I asked, 'Did you get it in the neck?'

He told me he had.

I couldn't resist one more little dig at the pre-flight briefing. I got up and asked, 'Has everyone got their passports?'

Then, that afternoon, we got on the plane and headed for Taji. By that time, we'd been on the trot for about 36 hours.

Despite the fact that we're trained not to talk about what we do, and we don't show our faces in public, working with the media on jobs like this was good. We managed them tightly, and they knew the drill. They wouldn't take any photos of us, and they didn't care about what we were doing. All they cared about was the prime minister's trip and what he was doing. They knew that they couldn't transmit anything until they got back to New Zealand. That was for their own safety as well as everyone else's. If word got out that the prime minister was there, there was always the possibility an attack could occur, so we had to avoid that at all costs.

*

On the second flight into Iraq, the weather was clear enough to get into Baghdad. We went out to the Presidential Palace and the Iraqi prime minister's office. When we turned up at the Presidential Palace, it was all singing and dancing, with all these people running around doing their thing. Prime Minister Key was led into this massive conference room. I'd already been in and checked it, and it had all looked good.

While the PM was having his meetings, I sat at the back of the room, just inside the door. The Iraqi guys had trays with mocktails on them that they offered to me. I just sat there, had a drink and got comms. As the meeting was wrapping up, I got warned by the security team to get out of the door first.

'I need to stay on the PM's shoulder and will follow him out,' I said.

'OK, then,' they said, and left me to it. They must have known what was coming.

I was walking behind John Key, just doing what I normally do. But, then I walked out the door and saw the Iraqi president Fuad Masum there, shaking hands with all the dignitaries as they left. He held his hand out to me, and what I should have done was just shake it – but I didn't. Instead, I said, 'Oh, sorry ...' and ducked past him, trying to make myself look like a minion. All the cameras from Iraq and the one from New Zealand were on me. It wouldn't have been a great look if I'd ended up on Iraqi TV snubbing their president!

When I got in the car, I said to the prime minister, 'So I can see why I should have gone out the door before you ...'

'Yeah,' he said, and cracked up laughing. 'Did you not know that was going to happen?'

I had to admit that I'd been warned about it, but I'd thought I knew best!

*

With the meetings concluded, it was time to fly the PM up to Taji. It was only about 30 kilometres to the northwest of Baghdad, but driving was out of the question because of the risk of IEDs on the roads.

They had a cameraman who was with us taking footage all the time. Whatever he shot got shared between the networks, because there was limited space on the aircraft. He was this young fella who was just following the prime minister around. I remember him standing up in front of us at an airfield while we were waiting for the helicopters to arrive, looking around. I walked up to him and said, 'Do you know what's going on there?'

He went, 'No.'

'No one's told you what our itinerary is?'

'No.'

'I'll keep you up to date as it happens, because it's about to happen. We're going to fly into Taji.'

'OK, cool. Thanks, man.'

'If there's anything you need to know, just let me know.'

On the flight, I could see him switching between filming the landscape below and filming the prime minister. It must have just been blowing this young guy's mind.

*

We finally arrived at Taji, 24 hours later than planned. The following day, the prime minister went out and observed the troops doing some training exercises, including how to locate and disarm IEDS, then he addressed the troops. When asked about Taji, he said, 'It's sort of a goddamn awful place, isn't it? It's desolate, it's sort of beige. It's a tough operating environment, and our people are out there working.'

Just how tough an operating environment Taji was got reinforced when we tried to fly out of there later that day. A couple of American CH-47s turned up to fly us out, and we could see there was a bit of a dust storm kicking up on the horizon. We got on the helicopters, which were full of gear that we had to climb over to get into our seats.

As we were flying along, the dust storm engulfed us. I could tell that we'd started to turn ... and we kept turning. I couldn't work out where we were going though, because I hadn't been put on comms with the pilot. I didn't know whether we were turning back to Baghdad or taking another deviation. Maybe the pilots were looking for an alternate field to land on? But no, we kept flying all the way back to

Taji. The pilots hadn't been able to get us out safely due to the sandstorm.

We had no choice but to wait it out, so we took the PM back to his accommodation and had a cup of tea. We sat there until about ten that night, by which time there was enough of a break in the storm for us to get out in the New Zealand Hercules.

*

As soon as we got back to Dubai, it was easy. We said our goodbyes, took a few photos, gave the PM a gift and handed him over to the New Zealand police's diplomatic protection team, and he went on his way.

And by the time I got back to New Zealand, the news had got out about the prime minister's secret trip – and who should be on the front page of the *New Zealand Herald* for a third time, but me. At least for the photo with John Key, they had actually blurred out my face.

14

HANDLING IT

OVER TIME, THAT PHOTO and the others that were in the news started to make me paranoid. I began thinking that people might be able to find out where I lived.

After we'd come back from Israel, Alia and I had bought a new house out in the country. Up until that point, I'd seen it as my sanctuary – but then I started thinking that it was so isolated that it would be the perfect spot for someone to come and target us.

The reality was that, if there had been someone in New Zealand looking for me, our security forces probably would have known about it. The logical part of my brain knew that, but the other part of my brain wasn't accepting any of it. Instead, I was thinking, *You look at Australia. You look at the Lindt Café siege. That guy said he was ISIS, but he wasn't. It could be anyone with a grudge who is mentally disturbed enough to try to take me on, or there could be people in New Zealand who are actively looking for me ...*

I was on high alert at all times. I was thinking, *If someone's going to come onto the property, they're not going to get the drop on me. I'll get the drop on them. There's just no way. If they're going to come up here, I'll put them in the dirt.*

Once again, it all came from having been in that threat environment for so long, then bringing those feelings across into my world outside of work.

When my paranoia was at its worst, I'd be out mowing the grass thinking about slinging my Ranger 223 semi-automatic on my back just in case someone tried to have a run at me while I was away from the house. We lived on four hectares, too far at times to get back to the house if something went down. It sounds abnormal, but it was just my body's survival mechanism telling me to be ready no matter what happened. When that sort of idea came up in my head, I had to really tell myself not to go through with it. I had to take a second and think, *I understand that you're saying that, but ...* Even though I felt like I needed to do it, I knew I had to put a stronger ideology in my head about what I was willing to accept and do. Effectively, I was using deradicalisation tactics against my own brain.

The SAS is a cruel mistress. She's highly demanding, and during my time it was definitely a single man's game. It's one of the hardest things you can do. To get there is blood, sweat and tears. To stay there is blood, sweat and tears – but the adventures you have are off the charts. You can go as hard as you want to, and the people beside you will take you there and beyond.

When you're in it, you're proud to be in it, wearing the belt and beret and flying the flag. When you're doing well, and you're getting reported on well, and you're getting to do a lot of epic shit, it just doesn't get any better than that for a young man. But it definitely takes a lot out of you, and it is a bit of a selfish existence. If you're a single man, sweet. You don't have to think about anyone else. But I wasn't a single man anymore, and I had someone else to think about. In fact, I had two people to think about: Alia and our newborn son.

Once I'd got commissioned, I'd felt like there was another career there for me and I'd have another ten or 15 years as an officer. I was really keen to do it, but I struggled to balance my career with my family life. For the first year after our son was born, I wasn't around as much as I would have liked to have been, because I was away doing officer courses and PPO trips.

While I was here, there and everywhere, Alia was at home by herself with our son. She felt isolated at our place in the country – and that replicated some of what she'd been through when she was kidnapped in Syria. It wasn't long before she started to feel really vulnerable and a bit paranoid there, too.

I tried to be home more, but it was just too difficult. These days, flexible working hours are an option, but back then the unofficial rule at work – especially as a troop commander – was that you'd be there after the boys had left, so maybe you wouldn't finish until six or seven o'clock. But I had to leave at 4.30pm, which I saw as leaving early. I had to go because Alia had stuff to do. She had to do her work and her study, and then it was my turn to be on with the young fella. In my mind, I should have been at work until seven o'clock every night, like every other troop commander was. Those expectations were both internal and external – I expected it of myself but I also thought other people expected it from me as well. As a result, my family took a back seat.

I used to get in my car at work and start getting pissed off. The closer I'd get to home, the angrier I'd get. By the time I got home, I'd probably be a nine out of ten, so I'd get in there and I'd find something to argue about. I'd basically just throw my shit on the floor and expect everyone to eat it. That happened for ages. I'm surprised Alia is still with me, to be honest. She's very resilient, but no one deserves that kind of stuff.

I'd have to fake being happy at home, but she could tell I was off. It was really sad, and it was really selfish. At the time, I resented her because she was taking me away from what I saw as my higher strategic purpose. Then I realised that was all bullshit. And once I realised that, I also realised how much of a selfish existence I'd been living for such a long time. I was expecting my family just to fall in line with my work. This was a me issue; I can't speak for all members of the regiment and their individual situations.

I realised I had to start taking into consideration that I had another part of my life – a part that needed my energy and focus on it, too. That was the hardest thing, because I'd been in the regiment for so long at that point. It had been everything I'd ever known and loved. But now I had to think, *What about these two? They will be there when you fall. The regiment will keep standing, but if you leave, who's there for you?*

Alia had pointed this out to me numerous times, but I had to come to that realisation myself. I didn't want to hear it until I was ready to get there myself.

*

While I was struggling at home, things weren't great at work either. I was away a lot and had additional courses to get across, plus I was completing master's-level studies – it was just one thing after another, and I was trying to keep on top of it all. Again, this was a me issue. I didn't have to take all those things on – I chose it. I was still just going hard all the time, and the cracks were showing. The stress was manifesting both mentally and physically, but I still was not acknowledging it.

Over the course of 18 years, it had been creeping up. My last two trips to Afghanistan had really taken it out of me. I'd poured my heart and soul into those operations. There was an element of performance punishment to what I was doing. In the regiment, they'll see that you're good at what you do, and they'll just keep loading you up and loading you up. As much of a serving as you want, they'll give it to you.

The responsibility is different as an officer because the buck stops with you. When you're a troop sergeant or troop staffy, you know the buck ultimately stops with the boss. There was also a lot more administrative work that had to be done for the troop. The tempo was much the same, but now it was ongoing. The memory loss and the fatigue were still there. Sometimes, I'd be in meetings and I'd be slumped down in my chair. Once, the OC picked me up on it and told me to sit up. I was that gone, I couldn't even sit upright. This was not normal for a professional soldier. I also noticed that, if I was talking to people – particularly people outside the 'circle' – I wouldn't make eye contact. I'd look away a lot because I was being guarded about the information I was giving them. I was happy to engage with them, but I wasn't really connecting.

For so long, I did everything I could to hide that there was something wrong because I didn't want to appear weak or seem like I couldn't handle it. It appeared everyone else was handling it all the time, and they had done since selection. It was one foot in front of the other, always moving forward, always handling whatever is thrown at you – pushing yourself to a state of failure.

The pain and suffering was part of the process in my eyes. I even wrote it in one of my notebooks at the time: *Enjoy the pain and suffering because it equals earnt rest.* I wouldn't feel like I'd earnt anything fun unless I'd smashed myself. Everyone was the same. By suffering, we felt we earnt the good things.

That sense of needing to endure in order to enjoy good things led some of the boys to tolerate a lot more from other people than they might have otherwise. Some of them stayed in toxic relationships because they had that mindset that they could handle whatever got thrown at them. They'd just say, 'I'm choosing not to engage with that,' and then handle the pain and suffering that came with it for ages. They had a high tolerance for suffering and discomfort because they'd been trained that way.

For me, I couldn't enjoy even small things that other people would take for granted unless I had absolutely hammered myself to earn them. It would feel wrong to just relax too much of the time; I'd have to go for a run or do something that depleted me in order to earn that relaxation. If I didn't do PT for two or three days, and I was just eating, drinking and sitting on the couch, I couldn't handle it. I'd have to go out and do something. Then, when I got to the end of it, I'd think, *I've earnt my sleep and I've earnt this burger and fries ... but don't rest too long ...*

I was in that operational mindset. I was always ready. At any given moment – and it happened so many times – we'd get the call, and we'd be out the door. Whether I was resting or not, I'd be registering threat all the time. Every time I went out, I'd be scanning. I'd be prepared.

*

One weekend, some mates and I went down to the Coromandel on our motorbikes. I always liked to go fast, and I rode a 2008 Harley Davidson Rocker that had a power output of 1600cc once tuned. I remember taking a corner really fast, even though there was a sign that said *Uneven surface up ahead*. My back wheel was in the air, and when it landed sparks flew off my exhaust as it hit the road.

I almost came off, but I just planted it and did the same thing on the next corner. There was nothing. I couldn't feel anything. There was no, 'Mate, you lost it there. You should slow down.'

Later, I put that together with the fact that I wasn't getting excited about jumping out of planes. I used to love parachuting, and I used to get such a big kick out of it. But I'd become numb to it. I felt like it didn't really matter at all. I realised there was nothing more hard-core than combat, and there was nothing more hard-core than being shot at. Not almost totalling my motorbike. Not jumping out of a plane by day or night.

All of that combined made me realise that something was wrong. And I knew I needed to do something about it.

*

I knew there were still plenty of opportunities for me in the regiment, and I was definitely going to get tested. But I'd already been there 18 years. I looked back on all of the stuff I'd done and wondered what else I needed to prove.

Who was I proving myself to? Was it myself to myself, or was it myself to others? It wasn't an easy thing to work out. My thoughts flip-flopped all over the place: *My son has arrived. I'm burnt out. But I made the commitment ...*

I talked to senior members on multiple occasions about how they managed to balance work and having a young family. They all said the same thing: they all wished that they'd had more time with their kids when they were younger. They all regretted not having done that. I thought about that, and I wanted to make sure that I was available for my son. I didn't want to have those same regrets.

Alia was doing her PhD at Waikato University, focusing on the concept of resilience, and she was highly ambitious. I'd be coming home and she would have spent the day with our son after being up feeding him at night. She was using the nights when I was home to work on her PhD. I felt like I was holding her back. I should have been there, but I wasn't there enough. I can't take that back. I wish I had been there. It was tough for both of us. The fact that I wasn't around was hard.

I realised I needed to step up more, and to do that I had to leave the regiment.

*

It was the middle of the year, and I hated the idea of leaving then, but I knew if I didn't leave then I wasn't going to go at all. So, on Monday morning, I went to see the CO and told him I was putting my papers in because I was burnt out and I felt I'd pretty much done everything I needed to do there. He offered for me to do reduced hours, and a few other options to suit my situation, but I said I wanted to do the job justice. He understood that. And a few days later, the OC called me into his office and said, 'Hey, Jamie, you've got long-service leave, which is three months. That covers your notice period, so you can leave next Monday. Can you handle that?'

'Yeah,' I said. 'I'll be right.'

I tried to do as much as I could in that last week. I got everything ticked off on my march-out form, which clears you off the system – it goes through every department to make sure they know you're leaving and that you've handed any gear back.

I also did my last jump out of the back of a C-130. It was a night jump at 12,000 feet with the rest of Air Troop.

Night jumps – by virtue of our load-out, approach to the landing zone and minimal landing-area markers – are one of the riskiest and most complex infiltration techniques in the regiment. That's why Air Troop is regarded as the most proficient troop in the squadron.

We all stood in a line on the back of the ramp, in full equipment (packs, webbing, rifles, helmets, NVGs), and the only light inside the aircraft was a dull red. The strobes on top of our helmets were on and flashing, and everyone was getting ready.

Then the green light came on.

I was the last man out. Standing on the ramp, I didn't register anything. I felt nothing.

I knew at that point that I'd definitely made the right decision. It was go time.

15

WHAT NOW?

THEN IT WAS JUST radio silence. I didn't hear from anyone. I didn't have to turn up on Monday. It was all over, and I was sitting there thinking, *What do I do now?*

It was mid-2016 when I left the regiment, and I'd love to say that doing that fixed everything ... but it didn't. To begin with, I was OK. But as the weeks went by, I slowly realised that I was gone. Actually gone. For the first time in 20 years, I didn't have the boys right there anymore.

I tried to fill the void by staying in a routine. Once I'd completed my bachelor's degree, I went straight on to studying for a Master's in International Security through Massey University in Auckland. I made that my focus after I left the regiment.

Alia was working full-time, and our son was going to day care three times a week, so when he was at home I'd look after him. When he was at day care, I'd get into it and work at the same speed and with the same intensity as I had in the regiment. I was trying to keep that same tempo going, just in a new arena.

I got into my operational rhythm: go to the gym, go for a run, go study, go get my son. Rinse, repeat. At the gym, I'd do an hour-and-a-half session, just smashing it all the time – going hard on the rower, lifting weights – because that's what we always did in the regiment. Then I'd head out for runs, covering 10–15 kilometres or more on the road and up in the Hunua Ranges. And when I got home, I'd do the same thing on the computer – go hard. Then I'd be looking after my son. Then the whole routine would start over again, round and round, day after day.

At the same time, I was still trying to figure things out. I noticed that when I went out on my long runs, I'd have these really dark thoughts. If I was running and someone came walking towards me, I'd think, *If that guy does something, I'll do this!* If there was no one around, I'd think about situations overseas and what I'd do if I found myself in them, rehearsing them in my head. That was just my training – being aware of my surroundings and registering threats, then doing something about it was what ensured survival for me and my team. But back in New Zealand when I was out running, I didn't need to protect myself or anyone else to that level. I'd always loved running, but I started drawing on that negative energy to motivate myself. I was using the anger, frustration and aggression to perform physically. As a result, everything felt dark and, by the time I got back from a run, I'd always feel angry.

I was still very much in that dark space where I kept thinking maybe I needed to have a rifle under the bed, ready to go. I'd catch myself in that train of thought and think, *What are you doing? Just chill out!*

But I couldn't chill out. I couldn't just automatically switch from soldier to civilian. It just doesn't work like that.

*

There was a lot of stuff inside me, and I didn't really know how to deal with it at the time.

Things weren't easy between me and Alia. She copped quite a bit from me. It was the same as when I had been at work and I'd get angry when I had to come home. I was still putting all my shit on Alia. She's a strong woman and she doesn't take shit from anyone, so when I gave her a hard time, she took it and then she gave it straight back. We'd both stand in our corners and box our way out, no matter what. We'd fight our way out to the very end. We've both got that staying power, so if it was anyone else I reckon they'd have been long gone. It took a long time for us to recover from that, to dial it back and to mend our relationship.

Her dad came to visit around this time, and we knocked heads a bit because he's quite a strong man as well. I was trying to find an outlet for what I was going through, but there was nothing there. I don't think my reaction would have been any different if I'd had a longer transition out of the unit, because I didn't have the tools to do things differently.

I began to recognise that things weren't right when I started to ask myself, *Why am I training like I'm going on operations?* And it was a sad moment when I really accepted that I *wasn't* going on operations anymore. Suddenly, I realised I wasn't that person any more. Once I'd accepted that, I thought, *All right, now what am I going to do?*

A lot of the guys get out and take on private security contracts in places like Afghanistan and Iraq. That feeds the beast for them. But I didn't want to do that. I left the unit for a reason – because of Alia and our son – so I knew I was going to have to take the hard path and do something different.

*

To begin with, I knew I had to make a conscious effort to catch myself when those threat-detection thought patterns kicked in, then deliberately put other thoughts in my head. So, if I was out for a run and starting down the paranoid-thought spiral, I'd remind myself, *Dude, you're just going for a run.* And I'd force myself to think of something else – big ambitious future projects, things I wanted to achieve in my life, concepts that intrigued me and I wanted to investigate. Anything, so long as it was positive. The more I thought about those things, the more excited I got about them – and the better I felt. But I had to switch the narrative and forcefully put myself in a different space. There was no change in my performance – I still ran the same distance at the same speed – but I felt a lot better before, during and after my runs.

It took about six weeks of actual, deliberate changing-the-narrative in my own mind whenever I went out for a run before those thought processes started to happen automatically. I still had to be mindful of not letting the negative ones back in, but gradually, every time I went out for a run, my brain would just go to thinking about future plans and I'd feel good. It was amazing when that started happening.

Now I know that by deliberately changing my thought processes, I was developing new neural pathways. It's a bit like gradually creating a new highway that your brain knows to take to get to where you want it to go. While that happens, the other neural pathways – which no longer serve you, so your brain no longer uses them – will get pruned back, and suddenly the change will start to happen without you being conscious of it. The timeframe for that process will be different for everyone. It takes as long as it takes. You just have to keep working at it.

*

Once I finished my master's degree, I got into doing some renovations around the house. Our son was now at day care five days a week, because he really enjoyed being with other kids, so I gave myself a six-month timeline, planned everything out and set about getting it all done. That gave me a bit more time to think about what I wanted to do afterwards.

Then one day out of the blue, I got a call from my friend Hutch. 'Have you heard about Steve?' he asked.

'No, what about him?'

'I think he's been killed in a helicopter crash,' he said.

I thought, *Nah, not Steve Askin. He's made of concrete. There's no way he'll die.*

I didn't want to believe it.

But unfortunately it was true. Huge fires had broken out on the Port Hills in Christchurch, and Steve had been involved in the fire-fighting effort. Then, on 14 February 2017, the monsoon bucket hanging from the chopper he was flying swung into his tail rotor, causing him to crash.

Steve's death was really tragic. He was only 38, and it was something I never imagined would happen. It really got me. That day I was talking to Alia at the dinner table and broke down in front of her and our son – something I'd never done before. It was just too much. Of all the people in the world for it to happen to, when there are so many other scumbags still walking around.

Steve was a top, top guy. He stood alone. In my eyes, he

epitomised the SAS soldier. Rough around the edges, but that was a good thing. Strong in mind and body. The kind of guy you want beside you in a battle. Guys like him are really hard to come by.

I went down to his funeral and seeing how many people he – and his wife, Elizabeth, and their two kids – had around them was heart-warming. His family had received letters and messages from people all over the world, but one in particular stuck with me. It was from a woman who'd been a guest at the Intercontinental. *I had hidden in a cupboard for six hours, and when I heard the insurgents going through the rooms below I realised that there was a high possibility I might not get out alive*, she wrote. *I never expected anyone to come in and save us, and no words can express the gratitude that I felt. Steve was a hero.*

Steve's mum, Leslie, reiterated that message when she spoke at his funeral, where his casket was flanked by a Mustang fighter and an Iroquois. 'It doesn't take going overseas and being an SAS warrior to be a hero,' she said. 'It's to do what's right. Be a hero to your family, your mates. Wherever you find yourself, choose to be a hero.'

*

After the funeral, and a few years later, the regiment also held a memorial at Papakura. The whole regiment was there, and we were invited to get up and share our memories of Steve. I'd spent so much time with him in the squadron, and we'd been through so much together, that I was definitely getting up to speak.

I told a funny story about Steve, then said, 'When I heard about Steve Askin dying, I broke down in front of my family —' and then the sadness just hit me. I had to stop to try to hold back the tears. Despite being close to Steve, I hadn't expected to get so emotional. I'd never seen anyone cry in front of the whole regiment, and it certainly wasn't something I ever thought I would do. *What the fuck is wrong with me?* I thought.

I had to take a minute to compose myself before I could carry on, and you could have heard a pin drop. It was pretty awkward.

Afterwards, I felt a bit shit about breaking down. Ricardo talked to me later and said, 'It makes the boys stronger when they see that sort of stuff. It brings them together.'

*

The fallout from Steve's death was tough. I thought about him often, and next thing I'd be crying in the car. I still think about him often. You can't wash those type of people out of your head.

Now, though, I feel him over my shoulder, watching me all the time. The thought of him drives me when I'm low. I can hear him say, 'Fucking hurry up!' and I need that. Sometimes, I can just hear him laughing in the background and that makes me feel better. It reminds me just to stick with it.

Steve's death helped me to feel gratitude that I was alive, doing stuff that I wanted to do. Nothing is forever and nothing is promised.

16

WHAT GETS YOU THERE

IN 2017, A MATE called Roger Mortimer got in touch. He was connected to the rugby league world, and wanted to know if I'd be interested in working with the Kiwi team as they headed into the World Cup. I said yes. I knew this was the right direction, and would start the journey away from my former self. When life presents opportunities, it's up to us to grab them and see where they take us. This was one of those situations.

And so I found myself working with players like Jared Waerea-Hargreaves, Simon Mannering, Roger Tuivasa-Sheck and Shaun Johnson. I told them right at the beginning that I didn't know anything about rugby league – but that wasn't what I was there for. I was there to look at how they operated as a leadership group, and do some one-on-one work with them and support the development of an enduring team culture. I spent five weeks with the team, right through the campaign, and they were working really well together and doing all the right things – but they ended up getting smoked by the Tongan team, who came out firing. When they got up, it felt like the whole of Tonga was inside Waikato Stadium, Hamilton. It was a great experience for everyone, even if we did lose!

It was during that World Cup campaign that I met Brian Smith, who is a bit of a National Rugby League (NRL) legend. Brian had played first grade and was the head coach for a number of prominent NRL teams. We got on really well, and he told me he'd be going to the Warriors as general manager of football in 2018. At the time, Stephen Kearney was the head coach of the Warriors, and it turned out he was after someone to look at their culture and do some leadership work with the players. So Brian Smith suggested he talk to me and Alia. Together, she and I had the experience and qualifications to be able to help with leadership and culture development in high-performing environments, and so, after talking to Steve, they sent us down to Papamoa for their pre-season training camp. There, we spent about four hours with the players establishing what they thought the team's culture and values should look like. There was quite a bit of clearing the air, with people really being truthful with each other, and there were a lot of good ideas to come out of it all.

Then, using a couple of other tools to establish and understand what the issues were, Alia and I formulated a plan for working with the team and getting them back together. We presented all that information back to the CEO, the GM and the head coach, and I said, 'If you want me to come in and start the process, I'd be happy to do that.' They put me on a three-month contract initially, and that turned into a year, then two years.

Sometimes, the players and I had to have some tough conversations, and that made people uncomfortable – but all I had to do was refer back to the stuff we'd agreed upon at the start of the year in Papamoa. The stuff about what the culture looked like and the shared values. The players had already told me what the pathway looked like, and they'd also told me to hold them accountable, so I didn't shy away from that.

And that year, the team did really well. They made the top eight, Roger Tuivasa-Sheck was the first Warriors player to be awarded the Dally M Medal for player of the year, David Fusitu'a was the NRL's top try scorer of the year, and Jazz Tevaga was named best interchange player. Not too shabby.

*

At the start of 2019, assistant coach Tony Iro decided that the Warriors staff were going to have a skinnies competition. In other words, we would have our skin folds measured at the start of the competition, then again in six weeks, and in that time we had to see how much weight we could lose.

At that point, I hadn't been training that much and I'd put on a bit of weight, although I was still a skinny prick – I was about 90 kilos, but was usually around 87. *Oh yeah!* I thought. *This will be good!* I had no idea it would change everything for me.

I reached out to a mate in Perth who used to be a bodybuilder. 'Hey, man,' I said. 'I need to do a shred programme. Can you help?' He gave me a nutrition programme and a training programme.

The nutrition programme was basically two to three meals a day consisting of good protein, carbs and vegetables. No alcohol, sugar, dairy, bread or crap carbs allowed. And drink plenty of water. That all made sense.

But when I looked at the training programme, I thought, *Is that it?* It was nothing – like, 30 minutes a day. I couldn't believe it. I asked my mate, 'Is that all for each day?'

'That's it,' he said.

'Are you sure?'

'I'm sure. I'm telling you, you'll lose about 1.5 kilos a week, which is healthy, and that's all you have to do. You're over 40 now, and you don't want to injure yourself. You'll keep your muscle mass, your cardio will stay up. You'll be good. You're not operating anymore, so you don't have to train like you are.'

I knew what he meant about injuries. I'd carried on with Brazilian jiu-jitsu, and had started to find I was constantly getting injured – hyper-extended neck and elbows – and it took me ages to recover. A lot of the guys who'd been doing it for a long time were not in good shape, and that made me reconsider whether it was smart to keep going. I'd been doing martial arts pretty consistently since I was eight years old, but I knew it was time to call it a day because it also kept me in that combat mindset I was trying to shift away from.

I started following my mate's programme on the Monday, and by Wednesday I felt completely different. I had heaps of energy because I wasn't training as much, and that was a revelation. I ended up winning the skinnies comp … and then I just carried right on with the programme.

What I found was that nutrition is a mood thing, it's an energy thing, it's an emotional thing. What you put into your body has a knock-on effect to how you think and feel, how you respond, how you work and how you get through the day. Eating well, moving well, sleeping well and thinking well are pillars that are all connected. If you're not eating well, you're not thinking well. If you're not sleeping well, you're probably not going to move well. If you're not thinking well, you're not going to sleep well. You can change how you feel, but you have to get those four pillars right in order to be able to do it.

Now, I can catch myself out when my thinking is starting to get a bit dark, and I know I need to change something to get those three things back into balance.

*

By the end of 2019, I felt the Warriors had it in hand. I was talking a lot less and we'd started opening up lines of communication, which is the baseline for high-performing teams. The player leaders had a voice, the players had a voice, and they were better connected to each other and the coaches, among other things. They had debriefs and feedback sessions, and they were more open in the way they talked after losses. And they had a mentoring programme in place. Things were looking good for 2020.

But then Covid hit, and with that the club's income dried up. I could see the writing on the wall, so I bowed out. Then I marked time for eight months, while Alia kept working. I've always made sure I have savings in the bank just in case, and that was definitely a just-in-case moment. It did, however, give me more time to read and work on myself.

While I was working with the Warriors, I'd read a lot of books on neuropsychology and how to change your neural pathways. The three key books for me were *Breaking the Habit of Being Yourself* by Dr Joe Dispenza, *The Happiness Hypothesis* by Dr Jonathan Haidt and *Into the Magic Shop* by Dr James Doty. Those three books were interconnected, and their key messages centred on the following ideas: the importance of meditative breathing; your ability to change the way you think and feel about things; identifying character traits that no longer serve a purpose; and learning to use the space between stimulus and response.

Meditative breathing allowed me to learn to stop and be fully in the present wherever I was and whatever I was doing. It helped me to clear my head and refocus my thinking. It's really useful when I wake up at three or four in the morning and my brain is going like a highway. When that happens, I focus on my breathing or I'll turn the light on and start reading a book. One or other of those things will help me to calm down, and I'll feel my heart slowing and my brain just dozing off, and I'll be asleep again.

Your brain does random stuff all the time, but you've got to keep plugging on and taking control of the way you think about things. You don't have to just roll with your thoughts and feelings. When your mind is on autopilot, if you feel angry, then you'll be angry. If you feel sad, you'll be sad. Or if you feel happy, you'll be happy. When you take control of your thoughts, though, you can question every single one that comes into your head. By doing this, you can change the script.

Slowly, over time, I've become aware of my thoughts to the point where I can keep watch over myself. I was a passenger on the bus for a long time, but now I'm the driver. It took a while to get from the back to the front, though!

*

In terms of character traits that weren't serving me, I had plenty of those – many of which had developed during my time in the regiment.

When it comes to the development of character traits, by the time you're 35 the stuff you've experienced throughout your life will concrete itself, and it's hard to undo that. I joined the army at 19 and the regiment at 21, and in those years all my attention and training had been focused on making sure I would survive on the battlefield and do everything I could to ensure that my team survived, too. That zero-to-hero response had been repeated over and over again until it became a character trait. It was so entrenched that I ended up using it inappropriately in normal settings – like when I was mowing the lawns, out running or arguing with Alia. During those times, I'd automatically go to the highest-level response. By being clearer about how I was thinking and feeling, I learnt to dial that all the way back so that my response was appropriate to the stimulus. But, again it took a lot of effort and repetition.

Another issue I had was with my expectations of others. In the regiment, those high expectations were drilled into us. But they didn't necessarily transfer easily to other parts of my life. In the regiment, if people didn't reach the expectations set for them, they'd be gone and you'd never have to deal with them again. Outside that setting, though, I couldn't just shut out people who didn't reach those expectations or standards.

I had to learn to recognise when my expectations were too high, then manage them accordingly.

There's a saying that there's a space between stimulus and response, and in that space lies our power: we get to choose our response, and that's how we grow. To me, that means recognising the emotion (because that comes first), then identifying the stimulus in the moment, and then questioning why you are being triggered. The last part is control over your emotion: pulling on the reins to slow things down, so you can reach a point of calm and understanding before responding. Again, getting to that point takes time and effort.

Once you recognise your own character traits, it becomes easier to recognise how you feel as the result of certain interactions. For example, there'll be some people who just rark you up. In that moment, you can learn to recognise what's happening, and think about how you're going to respond, rather than just reacting in the heat of the moment. You are in control of your emotional, mental and verbal responses in any given situation. Everyone has that freedom. Sure, you can still choose to yell at people – but you'll probably end up regretting it!

It took a while for me to figure all this out because I kept running with my operational mindset, running with the dark thoughts that would then manifest themselves physically. I had to stop myself and think about what was happening. *What are you doing? Are you going to stop on the side of the road and do five minutes of breathing and centre yourself? Or are you just going to keep manifesting this scenario that isn't even true and allow it to take you into a place of sadness, anger and frustration that just keeps going?*

Learning to recognise the space I was in at a particular point in time – and whether or not I could retrieve myself from it – was vital.

*

When the doors slowly started to open after Covid, Alia and I did some work with the New Zealand paralympic alpine ski team before the 2022 Winter Olympics. That was awesome. We spent two days with Adam Hall, Corey Peters and Aaron Ewen, and the first day was around individual stuff – self and leadership. Then we did some work around how high-performing teams operate. They were an awesome group, and they got right into it. And, between them, they won a gold, a silver and two bronzes at the games.

We also did some work with Triathlon New Zealand for the Summer Olympics. That came about through Hamish Carter, who was the GM there.

One of the key things I used to teach athletes was visualisation, and they'd get massive gains from it. I'd get them to visualise performing at their best, step by step, from the moment they arrived at their venue until the moment their event finished. The more colour, smell and realism they could put into their visualisation, the better it would work, as all the senses were being engaged. Then, when they went out to compete, things would fall into place, because they felt like they'd done everything over and over again already.

When I started reading about visualisation, I realised that I'd been doing it since I started skydiving. There, we'd mind-map the dive and do our formations on the ground, then once I got on the plane, I'd think through the formations. Once I jumped, I naturally followed through with the formations I'd practised in my mind.

*

At the start of 2022, my career took another big turn. I'd been doing a bit of work in the leadership and resilience space with Dilworth School students. The groups of boys we worked with were really engaging and intelligent, and they asked some great questions.

The philosophy of the school resonated with me. Basically, boys whose families do not have the means to provide their sons with a private education are selected to attend the school, and are given a scholarship that pays for everything they need during their journey from Year 7 through to Year 13. As long as they keep performing. The Dilworth Trust Board manages significant assets that operationalise the school and provide the scholarships. It's an amazing philosophy and opportunity for the boys who get selected.

Then, the school advertised for someone to become head of Te Haerenga – the school's new extensive outdoors programme. I realised that I had the skills to do the job, and I felt like it would be a great place to use my knowledge and experience. I was also really attracted by the opportunity to work with these young people, and to help them grow and develop. Their curiosity resonated with my need to constantly ask myself how things can be done differently or better.

Starting at the school was a little bit like being back in Kabul with the CRU in the sense that I spent a lot of time watching, listening and learning before I put any changes in place. It's something that's captured in my philosophy of 'what got you here may not get you there', which I've lived as I've learnt to switch from the mindset of the person I was to the mindset of the person I am becoming. I still find my brain trickling off into the distance with negative thoughts, and I continually remind myself that those negative thoughts just exist in my brain. I am creating them, so I can change them.

In this job, I've also had to take a good look at the values of the regiment that were so ingrained in me. I've had to work out how much they affect my life. No sense of social class distinction, humour and humility work well, but high standards of discipline in everything I do and the unrelenting pursuit of excellence can be misinterpreted outside of the military context.

It's taken me ages to get rid of some of that stuff. Learning to work within a different environment and space has helped me to practise being OK with things being as good as they can be. It's hard to learn to be patient, and to ride emotional waves in meetings and conversations with people. But now, when I catch myself thinking, *Oh, what are you talking about?* I realise that it's a place where I can do some practice. I sit there watching myself and trying to dial down my response.

It takes years to undo all that stuff. You've got to play the long game. You've got to be dead set on putting in the process to create a habit that allows you to better understand where you're at, so that you can change the way you think and feel about things any time you want.

AFTERWORD

ON ANZAC DAY 2022, I gave a speech at Dilworth about my experiences at the Intercontinental. That speech ended with these words:

> There can be no doubt that our nation's role in the wars
> and conflicts we have been involved in over the years
> has had a tremendous impact on New Zealand history
> and society. Above all, the terrible losses suffered by our
> country at Gallipoli and on so many other battlefields
> around the world have brought grief, loss and hardship
> to homes across New Zealand.
>
> What all these operations have demonstrated
> is the importance of the unique range of skills and
> capabilities that our Defence Force brings to the
> service of New Zealand. They have also shown
> that today's New Zealand military personnel, like

those who have gone before them, are dedicated to upholding New Zealand's national interests and the principles we hold dear.

This modern service doesn't come without costs to our men and women in the armed forces and to their families.

As servicemen and servicewomen, you choose to pay those costs. There are plenty of people who talk about doing it, who reckon they could do it, but the fantasy doesn't meet the reality because the reality is a big boy's game. It's not for everyone. You've got to *really* want it.

In the SAS, everything that you do is about saving lives. That's it. The whole thing. And you have to face the fact that your life will be put on the line at some point. Back when we went into the Intercontinental, and when the CRU went into Jan Mohammad Khan's house, we knew that the terrorists in those places had already killed a bunch of people, and would have no qualms about killing as many more as they could. In every operation, it came down to lives. How many more we could save? We always asked, *What can we do to get the terrorists focused on us? And how quickly can we do it?* We knew that the longer it took us, the more people would be killed and the more attention the terrorists would get. So we were fully focused on taking them out as quickly as possible, and weren't really worried about ourselves.

In Afghanistan, we didn't always know who we were going to run into. What we did know was that, if we wanted to have more than a temporary effect, we needed to go back and train the internal-security apparatus so the country could be self-sufficient into the future. But I was surprised at how quickly the Taliban took over in August 2021. That could have been handled a hell of a lot better. I have heard about international soldiers killing themselves over it, thinking that all they did there was a waste of time. It wasn't.

We provided a period of peace and security during which people could actually feel free for a bit, and maybe get educated and leave to go on to a better life. Meanwhile, those who remained in the country are suffering again, because they can't get out. The Taliban have turned the clock back once more, and that is what they were always going to do. They say they're being progressive, but their actions prove otherwise. It's sad to know that only 70 of the 200-odd CRU members I worked with made it out of the country when the capital fell. The rest were either killed or fled.

Ultimately, our armed forces are there to provide security and stability – to New Zealand, and regionally and globally with and to our partners. We do this so we can all prosper and grow as a global community. As for the NZSAS specifically? Well, what can I say that I haven't already said? Maybe I can finish by putting it this way. The selection course is just the beginning of a long, challenging and incredible journey. Along the way, if you manage to stay the course, you will develop the mindset and resilience required of a top-tier soldier. Survive, and you'll show yourself worthy of becoming a badged soldier or officer of the regiment. Getting there will drive you past your own limitations, and lead to incredible growth, but it will also take a toll – because nothing that's worth anything in this life comes without a cost. It's a journey that will stick with you for life. Who dares wins!

Acronyms

ANA	Afghan National Army
ANP	Afghan National Police
ANSF	Afghan National Security Forces
BDA	Battle Damage Assessment
CO	Commanding Officer
CRU	Crisis Response Unit (Afghan National Police counter-terrorism force)
EOD	Explosive Ordnance Disposal
HVT	High Value Target
IED	Improvised Explosive Device
ISAF	International Security Assistance Force
ISR	Surveillance and Reconnaissance (aerial)
JTAC	Joint Terminal Attack Controller
NVG	Night Vision Goggles
OC	Officer Commanding
PPO	Personal Protection Officer
RSM	Regimental Sergeant Major
SNO	Senior National Officer (NZ Army)
SSM	Squadron Sergeant Major
WODF	Warrant Officer of Defence Force